THE FULNESS
OF GOD

THE FULNESS OF GOD

*An Exposition of
Ephesians from the Greek*

by

JOHN H. CABLE

Member of the faculty, Moody Bible Institute

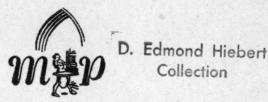

MOODY PRESS

153 Institute Place, Chicago, Illinois

THE FULNESS OF GOD

Printed in the United States of America

As "heirs together of the grace of life"
my wife and I unite in our deep appreciation of the treasures of truth in
Ephesians

To her, my companion and counselor,
I joyfully dedicate
this volume

FOREWORD

As the reader delves into this new volume on Paul's letter to the Ephesians, he will discover that its author has brought to his study of this profound and precious epistle, and to the writing of this book, a personal Christian experience that is mature and rich and mellow. A young, highly trained exegete could give one a fair approximation of the meaning of Paul's statements. But his book would lack that almost indefinable, yet clearly sensed atmosphere of "Christ in you, the hope of glory," as the great apostle expressed it. Someone has said that it takes a heap of living to make a house, a home. A like principle holds true in regard to the writing of a book. It takes a heap of Christian living to produce a book that breathes the atmosphere of our heavenly home. Dr. Cable's new volume on Ephesians does just that.

In addition to this, the author has brought to the writing of this book his long experience as an educator and a teacher. This is evident, not only in the clear and simple presentation of his material, but also in his application of the truth to the practical side of our Christian experience. Added to this is the fact that his wide reading down the years has enriched the teaching contained in it, with many apt illustrations. Finally, Dr. Cable has followed the Greek text as he has written this volume, with the result that its contents have been enriched and made clearer by the addition of many Greek words, their definitions, and the added light which they have thrown upon the English translation. Altogether, this is a good book, and the one who has had the honor of writing this foreword heartily commends it to the reader as a book that will enrich his Christian experience and ministry.

KENNETH S. WUEST.

CONTENTS

PREFACE

The material of this book has been prepared as I have taught the epistle of Paul to the Ephesians both as "English Bible" and "Greek Exegesis." Classes have never failed to appreciate our position in Christ, as set forth in the first half of the letter, or to be challenged to holy conduct as demanded by chapters four, five, and six. These class groups have encouraged me to prepare a manuscript which will take the form of a volume.

Of great works on Ephesians there is no lack, yet each author may feel that he touches a company who might enjoy his particular presentation. In writing these pages I have had three groups in mind: those who have been in my classes and desire to have samples of our study together in a crystallized form, those who may profit especially by direct exegesis from the Greek text, and those who read devotionally. These classes overlap.

While introducing about two hundred Greek words, spelled in English letters, I have attempted to save the work from seeming to be abstract or "over the heads" of those who do not work in this beautifully expressive language. An outline is placed at the end of each chapter, except the first, to aid the reader in getting the general plan before his mind. The alphabetical index of English words treated from their original meanings will be helpful for reference work. The volume would lend itself to use as a textbook for this "Prison Epistle."

Authorities are quoted, yet our chief dependence has been on the Holy Spirit, who has enabled us to work in the Scripture text with the aid of reliable lexicons.

A few subjects that are prominent in the thinking of our day are discussed and the Bible view presented. These include demons, capital and labor, divorce, race problems, and juvenile delinquency.

JOHN H. CABLE

11

Chapter I

INTRODUCING THE STUDY

Do YOU ever begin in the middle of a book? Some read the last chapter before they complete the others just to see how the story ends. If you were to begin to read the epistle to the Ephesians at chapter four you would be struck with the high expectations for Christians. We are asked to be lowly, meek, longsuffering, and forbearing. We are to be careful how we walk and guarded in our talk. All of life's relationships are put on a high plane. Husbands and wives are to live in love and sacrifice for each other. Parents are to train their children, who in turn must obey. Genuine service is to be rendered and employers should seek the welfare of their workmen.

If these ideals were realized in American life, divorce would be unheard of, child crime would disappear, and strikes would be no more. Singular, is it not, that our progressive civilization does not adopt the Christian way of living? We spend fifteen billions of dollars annually in apprending and prosecuting crime. To our shame, we lead the world in divorce. Juvenile delinquency is undermining our social structure, and on we go paying lip service to various creeds but giving life service to the devil.

But most of our citizens do not attend public worship. Millions of American children receive no religious education, and in some sections and among certain groups this condition is growing worse. The reports of four district superintendents of the Methodist church of the New York area indicate that there was a membership loss of 29,000, or thirty-eight per cent in the last fourteen years. In the last decade this, the largest communion, lost 760,000 Sunday school scholars.

And too many of our people are vocal in their cry of "hypocrite" to any who profess to be followers of Christ but do not "live up to it." "Hypocrisy is the homage which vice pays to virtue." There could be no spurious except for the fact of the genuine. And the standards of God's Word are attainable.

What is the secret of "a glorious church"? What will enable us to "walk not as other Gentiles walk"? The answer is found in the words of Paul's ultimate purpose in his prayer of Ephesians 3:19, "That ye might be filled with all the fulness of God." And this is not different from the expectation of the exhortation of 5:18, "And be not drunk with wine, wherein is excess; but be filled with the Spirit." Moreover this is really a normal Christian state when we remember that "the church . . . is his (Christ's) body, the fulness of him that filleth all in all" (Eph. 1:22,23). Professor Charles R. Erdman wrote:

"The fulness of God denotes the sum total of all His divine excellencies and perfections. The divine attributes such as omniscience, omnipresence, and omnipotence cannot be communicated to men. . . . With the virtues of God, however, men can be increasingly filled. These virtues are all embodied in Christ. As He dwells in their hearts by faith, these graces are increasingly communicated to believers, and manifested in them."

Since the church is the mystical body of Christ, it is only fitting that the individual members should properly represent the Head. Hence sainthood should be the rule among Christians rather than the exception. Our study of the first three chapters will show us just what we are "in Christ," and thus prepare us for the admonitions of chapters four, five, and six.

EPHESIANS 1:1-3

The salutation of the epistle, found in 1:1,2, implies spirit filled Christians. For Paul addresses "saints," *hagioi,* those devoted, and refers to them as "faithful in Christ Jesus." The authorized version might leave the impression that Paul addresses two groups, "the saints" and "the faithful," but the Greek text has no article before "faithful," *pistois,* so according to Granville Sharp's rule, the saints are faithful.

And observe that their sainthood is spoken of in connection with their place of residence, "at Ephesus," whereas their faithfulness is asserted to be "in Christ Jesus," the sphere of their spiritual lives. When, as Christians, we are true to Him whose name we wear, then will it be evident to our neighbors and friends that we are really devoted to the Lord. And the fact that "at Ephesus," *en Efeso,* is omitted in some important Greek manuscripts causes us to think of this book as a circulatory letter suited to any Christian church. Hence its teaching is more universally applicable. It challenges the devotion and fidelity of all. Its provisions and promises are for all. Its standards of conduct apply to all. No one who would please the Lord can embody less than "the fulness of God."

For these "saints" Paul wishes such "grace" and "peace" as emanate "from God our Father and from the Lord Jesus Christ." Peter characteristically would have these "multiplied" (II Pet. 1:1). It requires God to give grace. As Titus 2:11-14 teaches, God's grace brings salvation, sanctification, and an expectation of the Lord's return for us. How satisfying and sublimating is all this. Little wonder the gospel poet wrote:

> "Amazing grace how sweet the sound
> That saved a wretch like me;
> I once was lost but now am found
> Was blind but now I see.
>
> " 'Twas grace that taught my heart to fear,
> And grace my fears relieved;
> How precious did that grace appear
> The hour I first believed."

And "peace" comes with grace. Both emanate from God our Father and from Christ His Son who is the "Prince of Peace" and who, about to ascend from this earth, bequeathed to us His peace in the words, "Peace I leave with you, my peace I give unto you: not as the world giveth, give I unto you. Let not your heart be troubled, neither let it be afraid" (John 14:27). What a heritage! He was ever calm in spirit. He could bid the boisterous waves of the sea of Galilee, "Peace be still," and calm followed storm. He was never disturbed—not even as He was nailed to the cross, instrument of torture and salvation. Paul's wish for grace and peace for the Ephesian Christians can be realized only by their possessing the fulness of God. But this ideal is not impossible of realization since God, ever blessed, "hath blessed us with every spiritual blessing in heavenly places in Christ" (Eph. 1:3).

CHAPTER II

BLESSINGS THAT ABOUND THROUGH CHRIST
(Ephesians 1:4-14)

1. OUR ELECTION (1:4-6)

As WE consider the subject of our election by God the
Father, we do well to note that certain questions that are sure
to be raised by the thoughtful are answered in these verses. We
shall consider four of these.

a. THE GROUND OF OUR ELECTION.

Little wonder Paul begins this section of his letter with "Blessed
(is) be the God, etc." (1:3). Feeling as he does the wonder of
God's blessings, and not the least of these being His choice of us,
Paul praises God and especially as "Father of our Lord Jesus
Christ." "Chosen," *eklegomai,* a verb in the middle voice, means
to choose out from the others for Himself. Upon what basis did
God select us? We find our answer in the words "in Him."
We were chosen *in Christ.* As Principal Salmond writes in the
Expositor's Greek Testament, "Apart from Christ and without
respect to His special relation to us, and His foreseen work,
there would be no election of us." Or as Meyer says, "In Christ
lay for God the *causa meritoria* of our election." Pondering what
these scholars have said we are content to commit the profound
philosophizing on this subject to those who are minded to pursue
it further. We recall the lines:

"What a dot is the earth mid the orbs of the sky;
And compared with the earth what an atom am I.
Yet I with my mind's cobweb plummet would sound

That mind that knows neither fathom nor bound;
Would measure the depth of infinite decree.
Can a fly grasp a world, a shell swallow a sea?
I with my weak mind can do this and no more
I can worship and wonder, admire, and adore."

How marvelous that God chose us "in Him" who, when on earth, said to His disciples, "Ye have not chosen me, but I have chosen you" (John 15:16).

b. When We Were Chosen.

We were chosen "before the foundation of the world," *pro kataboles kosmou. Katabole,* "foundation," means to throw down as one does stones in laying a foundation. Hence the expression, "before the foundation of the world," suggests very, very long ago before this world was founded. In the eternal counsels of God we were chosen. Such a conception gives dignity to our Christian lives.

c. Why We Were Chosen.

Two answers are found to this question. In verse four we read, "That we should be holy and without blame before Him"; and in verse six we have as a second reason for His choice of us, "To the praise of the glory of his grace." In brief, these two statements head up in the ideas of our holiness and God's glory. Because He selected us, as a groom does his bride, therefore, we are intended to be holy, *hagious,* separated, and devoted to Him whose we are, and "without blame," *amamous,* not having any fault or blemish. How eager is the bride to be spotless in the eyes of her husband. The wedding gown must be free from wrinkle. But, alas, as we, His chosen ones, look upon ourselves, we say with the bride of the Song of Solomon, "I am black."

But since we realize that Christ, our heavenly Groom, has washed us and robed us in His own righteousness we complete the statement of Song of Solomon 1:5, "I am black but comely." Though "black" as I see myself in the white light of His revealing, convicting Word, yet am I "comely" to Him who has transformed me. And He says, "As the lily among thorns, so is my love among the daughters," whereas, I use a less striking contrast when I speak of Him and say, "As the apple tree among the trees of the wood, so is my beloved among the sons" (Song of Sol. 2:2,3). He outdoes us in expressing appreciation. Our heavenly Bridegroom sees us as we shall be when we experience the wish of I Thessalonians 5:23, "And the very God of peace sanctify you wholly; and I pray God your whole spirit and soul and body be preserved blameless unto the coming of our Lord Jesus Christ." Unfortunately we do not see Him as He really is. But there will come the day "when he shall appear" and "we shall be like him; for we shall see him as he is. And every man that hath this hope (fixed) in him purifieth himself, even as he is pure" (I John 3:2,3). The holiness of the church is Christ's aim. Are not the Christians of the New Testament period "called saints"? They are not "called to be saints" as the interpretive rendering of the Authorized Version has it. They are "called saints" because they are saints. Hence the instructions and admonition in the epistles to make for greater sainthood. Those "called saints" are the Corinthians, the Romans, the Philippians, and the Colossians. (See I Cor. 1:2; Rom. 1:7; Phil. 1:1; Col. 1:2.) In I Peter 1:15 we read, "But as he which hath called you is holy, so be ye holy in all manner of conversation (living)." Peter continues to tell why God requires this holiness of life by quoting Jehovah's words as found in Leviticus 11:44 (R.V.) "Be ye holy; for I am holy." Now this holiness is not simply a subjective experience, nor is it a doctrinal theory but a matter of practical daily living as Paul explains in I Thessalonians 4:3, "For this is the will of God, even your sanctification, that ye should abstain from fornication." The holy man is free from fornication and, of course, sinful practices without number, not mentioned here. We are chosen in order that we be holy.

It is easy to understand how those who are "holy and without blame" are "To the praise of the glory of his grace, which he freely bestowed on us in the Beloved" (1:6 R.V.). God's grace, *charis,* is His freely bestowed satisfying favor. To the Greeks that which satisfied was *charis.* Since beauty and symmetry were pleasing to them anything beautiful or symmetrical was called *charis.* When the satisfying benefits of the gospel were thought of there could be found no better word than *charis,* grace, to describe them; since grace comes from the Latin *gratia,* pleasing. The "glory of his grace" is that in God's grace which is resplendent since "glory" translates the Greek *doxa,* that which is seen or evidently manifest. When the sun is totally eclipsed, as we saw it in New York State on January 25, 1925, the onlookers behold a glorious sight as the light of the sun, called "the corona" or crown, shines forth. This is the "glory" of the sun. Hence the "glory of his grace" is that, in His free satisfying favor, which is striking. And what is more outstanding in the work of Christ for us than the forgiveness of our sins and the making of us to be new creatures? So our lives are to be "unto the praise of the glory of his grace." Now "praise" translates the Greek, *epainon,* which literally means, "a story upon." When a biographer writes the life of another he ordinarily praises or puts the best possible story upon the life that he writes. There once lived a Greek named Ulysses or Odysseus as the Greeks called him. He was a man of strength and bravery but would have died and been forgotten had not Homer, the poet, immortalized him. And we are to so live as to recount by life and lip the excellencies of the grace of God which were so freely bestowed upon us by Christ, the beloved Son of God. To this end God hath chosen us.

d. How We Were Chosen.

This is set forth in 1:5 in the words, "Having predestinated us unto the adoption of children by Jesus Christ to himself, according to the good pleasure of his will." "Good pleasure" translates *eudokian,* which literally means, "to think well." So our choice by God was not only His will but His enjoyment. He did not choose us grudgingly nor of some necessity apart from His pleasure, but He rejoiced to choose us, as does a suitor the object of His choice. "Predestinated," *proorisas,* means to limit or bound or determine before. Hence His choice of His children was predetermined. It was not a snap judgment but a deliberate, mature consideration. And observe the relationship into which this election of God has brought us as seen in the words, "unto the adoption of children." Adoption of children, *hyiothesian,* signifies that we have been put into the relationship of sons. What intimacy with the God of the universe!

2. OUR REDEMPTION (1:7-10)

a. How We Are Redeemed.

It is "through his blood" (1:7a), *dia ton haimatos.* This is the construction of the intermediate agent. Though our redemption was in the will of God, yet it required the blood of Christ to actually purchase us. "Redemption," *apolytrosin,* means release upon payment of a ransom. As Peter says, "Ye were not redeemed with corruptible things as silver and gold . . . but with the precious blood of Christ, as of a lamb without blemish and without spot" (I Peter 1:18,19). As Isaac Watts has expressed it in his majestic hymn:

> "Not all the blood of beasts
> On Jewish altars slain,
> Could give the guilty conscience peace,
> Or wash away the stain.

> "But Christ, the heavenly Lamb,
> Takes all our sins away;
> A sacrifice of nobler name,
> And richer blood than they."

Or as Dr. James M. Gray's great chorus has it:

> "I am redeemed, but not with silver,
> I am bought, but not with gold;
> Bought with a price, the blood of Jesus,
> Precious price of love untold!"

b. What Redemption Means to Us.

As we consider these verses we find in 1:7b, 8, 9 an answer to the question, What does redemption mean to us? Nothing less than "the forgiveness of sins." "Sins" here is *paraptomata* or falling aside or deviation from the path of rectitude. "Forgiveness," *afesin,* means sending away. So in the remission of our sins we are separated from the record of our wanderings from God and His way and truth. Redemption, *apolytrosin,* signifies that we who were once "sold under sin" (Rom. 7:14) have been bought back by Christ giving "his life a ransom for many" (Mark 10:45). Sin now has no dominion over us. We are not condemned before the law, but we rejoice in God's grace; yes, "the riches of his grace."

And if forgiveness of sins means so much to us, what does it mean as to our obligation to God? For one thing, He has put us under an everlasting debt of gratitude to Himself. The Christian system is unique in the matter of dealing with the sin question. Our debt of sin was cancelled by Christ's death.

> "Jesus paid it all,
> All to Him I owe;
> Sin had left a crimson stain;
> He washed it white as snow."

Certainly "He hath abounded toward us in all wisdom and prudence" when He "made known unto us the mystery of his will . . . which he hath purposed in himself." It was His will and His purpose that we should have free forgiveness. What a boon! Millions of penitents have rejoiced when they, like Bunyan's "Pilgrim," felt the load of sin roll from their backs as they saw the meaning of Christ on the cross.

> "At the cross, at the cross,
> Where I first saw the light
> And the burden of my heart rolled away;
> It was there by faith I received my sight,
> And now I am happy all the day."

c. What God Will Realize in Redemption.

Since our redemption is so precious to us, we do well to think of what God will realize in our redemption as stated in 1:10. Two expressions especially challenge our consideration, namely, "the dispensation of the fulness of times" and "That . . . he might gather together in one all things in Christ." Of the latter statement of purpose, the important term, exegetically, is the Greek word, *anakephalaiosasthai.* It is derived from *kephale,* the head, or *kephalion,* chief point or summation. Hence to head up or sum up would be the meaning of the term. The first three letters, *ana,* may mean again. This taken with the thought of the main part of the verb would give us the meaning to head up or bring together again. This all leads to the conclusion that God intends to realize again a lost pristine unity in Christ. Some scholars object to this idea, but as the Expositor's Greek Testament says, "If it (*anakephalaiosasthai*) does not itself definitely express the idea of the restoration of a lost unity it gets that idea from the context. For the whole statement . . . runs in terms of a redemption, and the cognate passage in Col. 1:20 speaks of a final reconciliation of all things." The verb form being in the middle voice signifies that God would have all things brought under Christ for Himself. Upon the baptism of Christ, the Father's voice from heaven said, "This is my beloved Son, in whom I am well pleased" (Matt. 3:17). Why should not God take pleasure in the headship of His Son who does always those things that please the Father? Many a military leader has had dreams of world empire through force. Jenghiz Kahn, Tamerlane, Nebuchadnezzar, Cyrus, Alexander, Caesar, Charlemagne, Napoleon, and Hitler are examples of overweening ambition. But "God also hath highly exalted him, and given him a name which is above every name: That at the name of Jesus every knee should bow . . . and that every tongue should confess that Jesus Christ is Lord, to the glory of God the Father" (Phil. 2:9-11). And Christ's redemptive work makes it possible for us to own Him as our Saviour and Lord as redeemed, blood-washed saints.

Now God purposed that this gathering together of all things heavenly and earthly in Christ should be "in the dispensation of the fulness of times." "Dispensation," *oikonomia*, administration or management of property. The figure suggested is that of a large household of which God is the Master. As such, He has an administration of the affairs of His house to His liking. The particular type of administration mentioned here is that of "the fulness of times" when He heads up everything under Christ. We observe that here, "times," *kairoi*, seasons or opportune times are referred to rather than *chronoi*. The latter means extent or duration rather than quality of time. In Galatians 4:4 we read of God sending forth His Son in the "fulness of time." When all was ready Jesus was born. But that event marked a particular "time," *kairos*, toward which all past time, *chronos*, marched. And Jesus will come to earth again. (See Acts 1:11; I Thess. 4:16; I John 3:2.) That will be another important season in the divine plan. Then will be realized the results of His redeeming love and Christ's redemptive work, His death and resurrection, when He "Who was delivered for our offences, and was raised again for our justification" (Rom. 4:25) will "see of the travail of his soul, and shall be satisfied" (Isa. 53:11). Little wonder Paul introduces this section of this epistle by saying, "Blessed be the God and Father of our Lord Jesus Christ." "Blessed," *eulogetos,* according to Lightfoot, "describes the intrinsic character" of God as praiseworthy. What He is and what He does, merit praise only and always. And His plan and program of redemption through Christ is most praiseworthy. Little wonder Zacharias, "filled with the Holy Ghost," prophesied saying, "Blessed be the Lord God of Israel; for he hath visited and redeemed his people" (Luke 1:67,68).

3. OUR INHERITANCE (1:11,12)

Though scholars differ as to the best translation of verse eleven, it seems reasonably clear that it should read in English as follows: "In whom we also have been taken as an inheritance, etc." In the Old Testament, God is referred to as the inheritance of His people. Likewise we have the companion idea expressed in Deuteronomy 32:9, "For the Lord's portion is his people; Jacob is the lot of his inheritance." But since through the unbelief of Israel we have obtained mercy (Rom. 11:30), all who believe in Jesus Christ as Saviour and Lord are God's inheritance. As Paul wrote to the Corinthians, "Ye are God's husbandry (tilled ground), ye are God's building" (I Cor. 3:9b).

a. How We Became His Inheritance.

In verses 11 and 12 we find the answers to two questions that might arise; namely, How did we become His inheritance? and why did He make us His inheritance? The answer to the first of these questions is that we were made His inheritance by His purpose and plan. We were "predestinated (to be this inheritance) according to the purpose of him who worketh all things after the counsel of his own will." His "will," *thelema,* is His inclination. His "counsel," *boule,* is His deliberated plan. Therefore, "the counsel of his will" is the deliberate plan which He feels inclined to carry out. Now God purposed, *prothesis,* placed before His mind to do this very thing, that is to make us His inheritance. And when God purposes and plans He performs. He "worketh all things after the counsel of His own will." History relates that Darius the Persian had his servant come before him at meal time and say, "Master, remember the Athenians." Thus Darius kept before his mind with deliberate and insistent purpose to attempt the destruction of the Athenians. Porcius Cato, the censor, never made a speech in the Roman senate without including *Carthago delenda est,* "Carthage must be destroyed." Little wonder there was a Persian campaign against Athens and a Roman campaign against Carthage. And little wonder the Lord laid siege to our hearts and won them according to His purpose. Little wonder we yield our all to Him who is our Lord and Master. He has willed it so, and we seek to ascertain and do His will. We do not resist Him.

b. Why He Made Us His Inheritance.

We have already suggested why He made certain ones to be His inheritance. The answer is, "That we should be to the praise of his glory, who first hoped in Christ." Both Vincent and the Expositor's Greek Testament are of the opinion that Jewish Christians who had had Messianic expectations are referred to as those "who first hoped in Christ." Any man's inheritance reflects credit upon him. And as the Shorter Catechism states, "Man's chief end is to glorify God." So whether Jewish or gentile Christians or both, they are made God's inheritance for His glory.

4. OUR PRESERVATION (1:13,14)

What of the doctrine of preservation? It were better to take the whole matter of security out of the realm of apologetics and treat it as a fact of Christian experience. This does not mean that the doctrine is without Bible basis. But it does mean that there are millions of earnest Christians "Who are kept by the power of God through faith unto salavation (which is) ready to be revealed in the last time" (I Peter 1:5).

a. OUR SECURITY.

Wherein does our security lie? "In Christ in whom ye also trusted." The author of Hebrews pictures the Christian's hope "as an anchor of the soul, both sure and stedfast, and which entereth into that within the veil; whither the forerunner is for us entered, even Jesus" (Heb. 6:19, 20). The poet has laid hold of this idea and written:

> "We have an anchor that keeps the soul
> Steadfast and sure while the billows roll;
> Fastened to the Rock which cannot move,
> Grounded firm and deep in the Saviour's love."

On the eve of his martyrdom, Paul wrote to his "dearly beloved son" Timothy, "For I know (*oida*, spiritual insight) whom I have believed, (and continue to believe, as the perfect tense suggests,) and am (have been) persuaded (and continue to be persuaded) that he is able to keep that which I have committed unto him (to guard my deposit of faith) against that day" (II Tim. 1:12b). For Paul there was no doubt as to his "making heaven his home." He knew Christ and was sure of his eternal securities. He trusted the vault of heaven.

b. HOW WE BECAME SECURE.

Since a sense of certainty as to ultimate salvation is a fact of consciousness, we might inquire as to how we did become se-

cure. The answer, so far as our part is concerned, is found in
the two verb forms "ye heard" and "ye believed." But the thing
heard and believed is important. "The word of truth" translates
ton logon tes aletheias, literally, the discussion of the truth.
Christ is called *"The Word"* in John 1:1. He expressed the
thought of God to us just as a word conveys an idea. Of Himself
He said, "I am . . . the truth." So it is easy to see how "The
Word of the Truth" could refer to the story of Jesus, otherwise
described here as "the gospel of your salvation," *to evangelion
tes soterias hymon,* the good news of your salvation. So the
story of Jesus is the good news by which we are saved. On our
part we must hear and believe this. And we are "sealed" only
upon such hearing and believing. And always and everywhere
"Faith cometh by hearing, and hearing by the word of God"
(Rom. 10:17).

But if we must hear and believe the gospel in order to be
"sealed," it is God's part in this process to do the sealing by "the
Holy Spirit of promise." And this is the divine order according
to the record of the early church as found in the Acts of the
Apostles. (See Acts 2:38; 9:17; 10:44; 19:2 *et al.*) And we find,
"sealed," to be a rendering of *esphragisthete,* a very interesting
word. In the Oxyrhyncus papyri we find frequent uses of it.
For example this: "I gave the letter sealed (esphragigmena) to
the messenger on the twelfth, etc." Moulton and Milligan see
that the idea here is sealing for security. In Matthew 27:66 the
word is used for "sealing the stone" in order to make the tomb
of Christ secure so that His disciples could not take His body
from the tomb as the chief priests and Pharisees suspected they
would attempt to do.

And in a spiritual way we are sealed by the "Holy Spirit of
Promise." Thus we are certified to be God's heritage by the
Spirit which was promised by the Old Testament prophets. (See
Isa. 44:3; Ezek. 36:26 *et al.*) And in another sense the Holy

Spirit's stamp or seal upon us is a promise of a greater fulness of blessing. Verse 14 says of the "Spirit of Promise," "Which is the earnest (*arrabon*) of our inheritance." *Arrabon* means something given in pledge of more to follow. In the papyri, mention is made of "a woman who was selling a cow who received 1000 drachmae as *arrabon*" (earnest money) until the whole was paid and the cow claimed.

c. WHY WE WERE MADE SECURE.

As in the cases of other blessings specified, viz., our election and our being taken for God's inheritance, so, in that of our security, the question of, why we were made secure, is answered by the expression, "Unto the praise of his glory." We Christians do well to remember that God's glory is paramount. Moses descended from the Mount of God's presence with a shining face which reflected God's glory. Peter, James, and John saw the glory of God in the transfiguration of Christ. The glorifying of God is demanded because it is essential in the very nature of the constitution of the universe.

CHAPTER SUMMARY

1. Our Election (vv. 4-6)
   a. The ground of our election (v. 4a).
   b. When we were chosen (v. 4b).
   c. Why we were chosen (vv. 4c-6).
   d. How we were chosen (v. 5).
2. Our Redemption (vv. 7-10)
   a. How we are redeemed (v. 7a).
   b. What redemption means to us (vv. 7b-9).
   c. What God will realize in redemption (v. 10).
3. Our Inheritance (vv. 11, 12)
   a. How we became His inheritance (v. 11).
   b. Why He made us His inheritance (v. 12).
4. Our Preservation (vv. 13, 14)
   a. Basis of our security (v. 13).
   b. How we became secure (vv. 13, 14a).
   c. Why we were made secure (v. 14b).

CHAPTER III

PAUL'S PURPOSEFUL PRAYER
(Ephesians 1:15-23)

TWO GREAT prayers are included in this epistle. The first is found in 1:17-23 and the second in 3:16-21. The late Doctor Kenneth Mackenzie was in the habit of using these two prayers as a benediction. The former, which we study in this chapter, has as an ultimate aim, our knowledge, and the latter, divine fulness in our lives. That we should pray is very evident. Jesus has bidden us to pray. He prayed. Blessings come through prayer. And "Satan trembles when he sees the weakest saint upon his knees." These two prayers referred to are Paul's.

1. THE PREREQUISITES TO SUCH PRAYER (1:15)

a. PERSONAL FAITH IN THE LORD JESUS CHRIST.

These are, personal faith "in the Lord Jesus Christ," and "love for all the saints." Only those who trust Jesus Christ to be their Saviour and are born from above and thus have become new creatures in Christ Jesus are capable of such knowledge as is referred to in verse seventeen.

b. LOVE FOR ALL THE SAINTS.

An unmistakable sign of the new birth is "love unto all the saints." As John says, "We know that we have passed from death unto life, because we love the brethren" (I John 3:14). Paul, therefore, limits his petition to those who have exercised faith in Christ and have manifested love for the saints because it would be futile to offer such a prayer for men in general since

"The natural man receiveth not the things of the Spirit of God: for they are foolishness unto him: neither can he know them, because they are spiritually discerned" (I Cor. 2:14). First things must come first. And it is just as impossible for the unregenerate to understand the things of the Spirit as it is for the uneducated Hottentot to understand Shakespeare.

2. THE PROMINENCE OF PRAYER AS STRESSED HERE (1:16)

a. PRAYER SHOULD BE "WITHOUT CEASING."

In I Thessalonians 5:17 we have *adialeiptos* which is, literally, not leaving off or "without a let up." The inclination might naturally be to cease from praying for people who had trusted Christ and manifested a love for other Christians. But with Paul this was the very kind of people for whom he felt obligated to pray. Maybe converts would get on better if pastors would supplicate for them more faithfully and fervently. John G. Paton, the great missionary to the New Hebrides, testified to the effect upon him, even as a lad, because he knew his father was praying for him.

b. PRAYER SHOULD BE "WITH THANKSGIVING."

In fact, this is the main statement of verse sixteen. Says Paul, I "cease not to give thanks for you." And "for you" is *hyper hymon* in Greek, which literally means, over you or for your sake or even instead of you. There is a suggestion here that these Christians failed to be sufficiently expressive on their own account; and the great hearted apostle, with the indulgence of a father, made up for their lack of thanksgiving. They did not fully appreciate to what they were heirs in Christ as did he. The partaking of the bread and the wine in holy communion is frequently referred to as the "Eucharist" because, as Matthew 26:27 records, "and he took the cup, and gave thanks (*eucharistesas*), and gave it to them." And ought not every blessing we enjoy from Christ be as sacred to us as the solemn feast of love which we experience in communion? If so, we will be of thankful hearts, and we will praise with our lips.

> "Every blessing we possess,
> And every victory won,
> And every thought of holiness
> Is His alone."

c. PRAYER SHOULD BE SPECIFIC.

Paul "made mention" of these particular Christians in his prayers. "Mention" translates *mneian,* from the same root as the Greek verb for remember. In the apostle's praying, there were petitions that dealt with particular needs of definite persons. It is heartening to call by name certain ones who need our prayers. A regular feature of the Sunday morning worship service of the great Moody Church of Chicago is the reading of requests sent in by those who ask for the prayers of the church. This is a sacred season as all present with bowed heads and loving hearts unite in silent prayer for specific requests. The writer, in a hospital awaiting a major operation the following morning, heard his name mentioned and his need presented at the throne of grace by a missionary brother from the pulpit of this church. This was stimulating to faith as one realized that thousands said "Amen" to this prayer. In his "Ministry of Healing," Dr. A. J. Gordon reminds us of the difficulty of exercising faith as an individual if the church as a body fails to believe. He says that it is futile to hold up a handkerchief if the crew will not hoist the sail. But when the church definitely supplicates for clearly defined matters we are encouraged to believe that prayer is answered.

d. Prayer Should be Corporate.

"Prayers," renders the word, *proseuchon,* which is applied to the "prayer meeting." In this type of meeting the one leading in prayer prays with the others who pray together with him. Hence corporate prayer should be audible and interpretative of the desires of all present.

3. THE PURPOSE OF PAUL'S PRAYER—"THAT YOU MAY KNOW" (1:17-23)

a. God Grants this Knowledge.

"Knowledge is power" is a statement trite but true. A generation ago college presidents regaled the students with the economic value of each day's attendance at college—about ten dollars; not such an attractive sum in our era of billions. The idealists speak of "Knowledge for knowledge's sake." Wrote Tennyson in "In Memoriam":

> "Let knowledge grow from more to more
> And more of reverence in us dwell,
> That mind and soul according well,
> May make sweet music as before
> But vaster."

In this life we are keenly aware of our limitations as to knowledge. This Paul admits when he says, "Now I know in part; but then shall I know fully even as also I was fully known" (I Cor. 13:12 R.V.).

As to the knowledge referred to, we note God gives this knowledge.

Ordinary knowledge is acquired whereas wisdom is a gift (James 1:5). God has made us sentient beings with capacity for knowledge. But because of the nature of this knowledge together with the unusual method of attaining it, we receive it as a gift from Him.

b. This Knowledge is Spiritually Comprehended.

Paul prays, "That the God of our Lord Jesus Christ, the Father of glory, may give unto you the spirit of wisdom and revelation in the (full) knowledge of him" (1:17). In I Corinthians 2:6-10 we read: "We speak wisdom among them that are perfect (*teleiois*, initiated, mature): yet not the wisdom of this world. . . . But we speak of the wisdom of God in a mystery . . . Eye hath not seen, nor ear heard, neither have entered into the heart of man, the things which God hath prepared for them that love him. But God hath revealed them unto us by his Spirit." So God gives, as Paul prays, a spirit of wisdom (*sophia*, full intelligence so as to be able to use knowledge aright) and revelation (*apocalypsis*, an uncovering so as to lay bare what has been concealed). In brief, He gives us a wise and revealing spirit. And this spirit is to operate within the sphere of the knowledge (*epignosis*, full knowledge) of God. God's field of knowledge is vast as compared to our limited sphere.

c. The Realization of this Knowledge Requires an Inward Miracle.

Since a miracle is the result of a personal power coming from without and working the unusual, we do well to note that God is here referred to as "the God of our Lord Jesus Christ, the Father of glory." On the cross Jesus asked the Father, "My God, my God, why hast thou forsaken me?" But here God is also termed, "the Father of glory," or glorious Father. This speaks of the radiance of His character. From Him emanate gifts and graces that convey to us divine blessings as the rays of the sun carry light and heat, health, and happiness to our world. And not the least of these blessings is the gift of spiritual insight as expressed by "The eyes of your understanding being enlightened" (1:18). "Understanding" translates *kardias,* heart. And "heart" in the Scriptures means the whole self, the personality, or the soul. It is the inward being. Hence our expression speaks of the illumination of the eyes of the soul. Being born again, becoming a "new creature" in Christ, ought to carry with this experience the creation of members and abilities corresponding to those with which we are blessed in our natural bodies. If natural generation's product is wonderful, ought not the birth "from above" (*anothen,* John 3:3) be altogether glorious? And here special mention is made of the quickened eyes of the soul. "The eye is the window of the soul." A sparkling eye reflects an alert spirit. Recall Jonathan's enlightened eyes when he had eaten of the forbidden honey and see with what slaughter he laid the Philistines low while "the people (of Israel who had not eaten of the honey) were very faint" (I Sam. 14:27-45). When the glorified Christ is portrayed in Revelation 1:13-16, "his eyes were as a flame of fire." What penetration! May this prayer of Paul's be answered for both writer and reader of these lines. May our spiritual eyes be enlightened. The purpose of this inward illumination is "that you may know." The Greek word for know in this place is *eidenai,* to perceive directly. The perception rather than the process of seeing is stressed. The form is a perfect tense and therefore means to have seen and so to know. And evidently it is an intensive perfect and stresses "existing results." Therefore it signifies to have come to know and to continue to know. Such knowledge as we shall now consider should ever be in mind.

d. The Content of this Knowledge.

There are three things specified as included in this knowledge that Paul would have us possess, namely: "The hope of his calling," "the riches of the glory of his inheritance in the saints," and "the exceeding greatness of his power toward us-ward who believe." The apostle desires us to know "what" each of these means. And we may ask just what is meant by each.

(1) *"The hope of his calling."* Hope is desire plus expectation. The baby robin with open mouth, as its mother alights by the nest with its morning worm, is a picture of hope. It desires and expects food. Hope goes with faith in the initial stages of Christian experience and should persist until we see Him face to face. These Ephesian Christians "who first trusted in Christ" "should be to the praise of his glory" (1:12). Sinners "having no hope" (2:12). But Christians enjoy "the hope of salvation" (I Thess. 5:8). We enjoy "the hope set before us . . . as an anchor of the soul, both sure and stedfast" (Heb. 6:18,19). And as I John 3:3 tells us, "Every man that hath this hope in him (upon Him, *epi auto*) purifieth himself, even as he (that One, Jesus) is pure." Peter bids the "elect," (I Pet. 1:2), to "hope to the end" (I Pet. 1:13). And Paul classes hope with faith and love which abide (I Cor. 13:13).

Our minds are directed to a peculiar hope, "The hope of his calling."

First Corinthians 1:26,27 teaches us "that not many wise men after the flesh, not many mighty, not many noble, are called: But God hath chosen the foolish . . . to confound the wise." Little wonder that we think of the "hope of his calling" since we are hopeless apart from His call. But his choice of us which comes as a clarion call to discipleship and duty carries with it hope. This explains the eagerness of the Christian to realize God's purpose for his life and the energy of the Christian worker to be instant in season and out of season in service.

And Paul prays that the chosen, redeemed, sealed ones may "know" just what this hope is. Matthew 13:14 (R.V.), quoting the prophet Esaias, speaks of those who "seeing . . . see and (do) not perceive." "Perceive" translates the same Greek root, *id,* as is translated "know" in Ephesians 1:18. And perception is interpretation. It is reading meaning into sensation. It is appreciation. So Paul would have us appreciate the hope that we cherish because we have been called by God. He was never the same after he was called by name on the Damascus road. (See Acts 9:4,5,6; 26:13-20.)

(2) *The value of the saints.* Then we should also know "The riches of the glory of his inheritance in the saints." This is the second thing that Paul would have us know. In verses 11 and 12 we see that we have been taken for God's inheritance in order that we should be to the praise of His glory. This is true both of Jewish Christians, as Vincent and others say, and also of Gentiles whose "hope is built on nothing less than Jesus' blood and righteousness."

By analyzing the expression, "The riches of the glory of his inheritance in the saints," we will come to know its meaning. This epistle is addressed "to the saints . . . even the faithful in Christ Jesus" (Literal translation of 1:1 according to recognized rules of Greek Grammar). Hence "saints" are "faithful" ones. The Greek term *hagioi,* "saints," carries the idea of separated from the mass of mankind. So saints are devoted. They really "belong" to God as love slaves. They love the Lord with all their heart, soul, mind, and strength. Broadus gives "piety" as the first requisite to a preacher. Every saint is pious.

Now God's "riches" (Greek *ploutos,* wealth) "in the saints" can be appreciated to a degree if we consider the price He paid for their redemption. Says I Peter 1:18,19, "Ye were not redeemed with . . . silver and gold . . . But with the precious blood of Christ, as of a lamb without blemish and without spot." To convey some idea of the vast wealth of King Solomon it is stated that "The weight of gold that came to Solomon in one year was six hundred threescore and six talents of gold." His riches and glory and wisdom amazed the Queen of Sheba who uttered, "The half was not told me" (I Kings 10:7). We who deal in tens, hundreds, and thousands can hardly imagine the value of billions of dollars. Much less do we realize the riches untold of God "Who holdeth the wealth of the world in His hands."

But His most precious treasures, as we judge, are "the riches of the glory of his inheritance in the saints." Moses told Israel that God had taken them out of Egypt "to be unto him a people of inheritance" (Deut. 4:20). Peter styles Christians, "a people for God's own possession" (I Pet. 2:9 R.V.).

But if we are His inheritance, just what is "the glory of his inheritance (as found) in the saints." A clue is found in I Corinthians 11:15 where a woman's hair is said to be "her glory." Says the Expositor's Greek Testament, "Her beauty has in her hair, its crown." Her hair makes her attractive to man, but Paul argues that she should be covered with a veil when she prays to God. Evidently God sees the heart, not the physical beauty, and in His presence her modesty is an asset. But her hair (Gr. *kome*, hair as an ornament) is the most striking feature of her attractiveness. "Glory" translates *doxa*, from *dokei*, it seems. Hence the glorious is the seemly, that which shines forth as the corona of the sun in the case of an eclipse. In chapter 5:25-27 Paul is discussing the church as related to Christ as a bride is to her groom or a wife to her husband. He says, "Christ also loved the church, and gave himself for it; That he might sanctify and cleanse it with the washing of water by the word, That he might present it to himself a glorious church, not having spot, or wrinkle, or any such thing." With what pains is the bridal dress prepared for the wedding day. It must be perfectly clean and kept free from spot or wrinkle or any such thing, and this immaculate attire bespeaks holiness of character. Now Christ gave Himself "for" (*hyper*, instead of) the church when He tasted death for her so

that He might present her to Himself a glorious church. And
her glory is in her purity and readiness for her heavenly bridegroom.

(3) The power of God. "And what is the exceeding greatness
of his power to us-ward who believe." This is the third bit of
knowledge that Paul would have us possess. "His power!" What
is it? The Greek *dynamis,* here rendered "power," means inherent power in manifestation as in the case of miracles. So when
the miracle is thought of as a sign of unusual power it is called
dynamis. Behrends once said "Miracles are incandescent points
in the throbbing circuit of the supernatural." Just as the electric
current is seen where it glows in the bulb so God's power is manifest in the extraordinary occurrence called miracle, *dynamis.* And
what greater miracle could be cited than the resurrection of Christ
from the dead referred to in verses 19 and 20? Other miracles
were just as truly wonderful works but that of Christ's resurrection is essentially a part of the "gospel" which a person must
believe in order to be saved (See I Cor. 15:1-4). The preaching
of the apostles contained the resurrection of Christ. In fact, without the resurrection there would be no gospel. "If Christ be not
risen, then is our preaching vain, and your faith is also vain"
(I Cor. 15:14).

And this power of God is for us, *eis hemas,* who believe. Let
us study together the words used to help us to estimate this power.
First, we read of "the exceeding greatness of his power." "Greatness," *megethos,* is frequently used as a title of excellence in the
Greek of the first century; as we speak of his highness, etc. And
"exceeding," *hyperballon,* comes from *hyper,* over, above, or beyond and *ballo,* to throw. Hence to throw beyond or to excel in
throwing. So we are led to contemplate the greatest possible
power. And in order to aid us in comprehending the magnitude
of this might, Paul adds "according to the working of his mighty
power," etc. Here we have three Greek words for power which

cumulatively present a picture of power. Here we have assembled the greatest array of terms for power that can be found in the New Testament. *Energeian,* from which comes energy, signifies the efficiency of power; *kratous,* has reference to applied power and, *ischyos,* to the endowment of power. Therefore we translate 1:19, "And what is the surpassing greatness of his power, unto us believers, as measured by the efficient force of his applied might."

A homely illustration of the aggregate meaning of these Greek words for power may be taken from the days when the animal wagons of the circus were drawn by horses. Fancy one of these heavy wagons stuck in the mud. The horses pull in vain. They cannot budge it. So they bring out Jumbo, the elephant. He is the embodiment of might. Where he places his monstrous head against the wagon it is applied power and the result is power at work. So the erstwhile stalled wagon moves out of the mud hole by the working of the strength of the elephant's might.

If we could so sublimate this mundane portrayal of power harnessed and hitched so as to picture to ourselves God's power moving the mountains of our life problems, we would have abundant occasion to rejoice with exceeding joy. As verse twenty continues, "Which he wrought in Christ, when he raised him from the dead." Christ was actually dead. God's power raised Him out from dead, *ek nekron.* Dead remain dead. This is a rule of nature. But here is something above and beyond the natural. This is supernatural.

We are prone to view life's situations as unaffected by the omnipotence of God. The miraculous is the unusual and hence the unexpected, the surprising. The customary continues. So we count upon only natural or ordinary causes to operate in our lives and experiences. But lo, the inspired writer would have us who are believers know "what is the exceeding (surpassing) greatness of his power." We should see the potential miracle before it happens for faith is the title deed of things hoped for (Heb. 11:1). And our faith will be strengthened as we behold God's power as manifest in Christ.

But God's power is manifest in Christ not only risen from the dead but also in Christ seated "at his own right hand in the heavenlies." Of the former we have "many infallible proofs" (Acts 1:3). The fact of the resurrection of Christ is attested beyond successful contradiction. (See I Cor. 15.) But as to the session of Christ we must have faith. As we read in Hebrews 9:24, "For Christ is not entered into the holy places made with hands, which are the figures of the true; but into heaven itself, now to appear in the presence of God for us." And again in Hebrews 10:12,13, "But this man, after he had offered one sacrifice for sins forever, sat down on the right hand of God; From henceforth expecting till his enemies be made his footstool." Hebrews 1:3 connects His deity, His substitutionary sacrifice for our sins, and His session. And Christ's being in the presence of the Father assures us of His intercession for us. Recall the scene of Stephen's martyrdom as recorded in Acts 7:51-60. He had called the Jewish leaders "stiffnecked and uncircumcised in heart"; he had told them, "Ye do always resist the Holy Ghost." They were "cut to the heart," and "they stoned Stephen." But his reaction was Christlike as he said, "Lord, lay not this sin to their charge." How account for this? By his vision of "the Son of man standing on the right hand of God." Was Christ, as Stephen's intercessor, "standing" to plead the cause of the Lord's servant who was in distress though He customarily sits in His Father's presence? It would seem so.

And may not we rely upon the protective power of our risen, ascended, and seated Saviour? He is "far above," *hyperano,* above in position every potentate and power which exists, *en to aioni touto,* in this age and the next. In 6:10 we are reminded or informed that it is with "principalities and powers," etc. that "we wrestle." *Pale* implies a contest of some duration with the participants rather evenly matched so that they tug and tussle until one can throw and hold down the other. But even if we must "wrestle" with these powerful personalities in the spirit world, yet Jesus is "far above" them all. They are "under his feet." And He is "head" over all things. Verses 22 and 23 present Christ as having a twofold headship. The order of the Greek text is instructive. It is as follows: "And him (God) gave a head over all things to the church, which is his body." Evidently this means that "the God of our Lord Jesus Christ, the Father of glory" gave to the church, as her head, Him who is Head over all things. But there is this difference, that Christ's relationship to the church is intimate and vital as is that of the head to the human body, while in the case of Christ's relationship to "all things," He is as a president or overlord.

An explanatory appositional word closes verse 23, "the fulness of him that filleth all (things with or by means of all)." His body, the church, is His "fulness." *Pleroma* is generally accepted as signifying that which is filled. Then we think of the church as having Christ formed in it by the Holy Spirit and thus representing Christ to the world as my body coordinated with my head reflects my personality. So the body is the *pleroma* or the "complement" of the head. How this conception dignifies the Christian personality. As the Psalmist says, God dwells not only in the high and holy place but also in the meek and contrite heart. Yes, "your body is the temple of the Holy Ghost" (I Cor. 6:19). As Paul wrote to the Philippians, "To me to live is Christ." So we Christians should know that the same Christ that died on a cross on Golgotha's hill now lives in us to empower us to live holy and godly in this present evil world.

CHAPTER SUMMARY

1. The Prerequisites to Such Prayer (v. 15)

    a. Personal faith in the Lord Jesus.
    b. Love for all the saints.

2. The Prominence of Prayer as Stressed Here (v. 16)

    a. Prayer should be "without ceasing."
    b. Prayer should be "with thanksgiving."
    c. Prayer should be specific.
    d. Prayer should be corporate.

3. The Purpose of Paul's Prayer—"That You May Know" (vv. 17-23)

    a. God grants this knowledge (v. 17).
    b. This knowledge is spiritually comprehended (v. 17).
    c. The realization of this knowledge requires an inward miracle (v. 18a).
    d. The content of this knowledge (vv. 18b-23).
        (1) "The hope of his calling" (v. 18).
        (2) The value of the saints (v. 18).
        (3) The power of God (vv. 19-23).

CHAPTER IV

IN THE HEAVENLIES IN CHRIST
(Ephesians 2:1-10)

IN CHAPTER ONE we learn that God "hath blessed us with all spiritual blessings in heavenly places in Christ." We have been chosen, redeemed, and sealed. The eyes of our hearts have been illuminated so that we now see spiritual values. Christians comprise the church, an assembly called out from the world to make up the body of Christ. But what were we before we were thus exalted to our present place in Christ? This second chapter opens with a reminder and description of our preconversion state.

1. WE "WERE DEAD IN TRESPASSES
AND SINS" (2:1-3)

In death the normal functions of the body have ceased because the soul has departed. Therefore, in the case of the dead, there is a separation of soul and body. And in the case of spiritual death, there is a separation of the soul from God. Our text here speaks of three factors that make for our being dead in trespasses and sins. They are "this world," "the prince of the power of the air," and "the desires of the flesh and of the mind." These separate us from God.

a. SEPARATED BY THE WORLD.

We are separated from God by the world, our general environment, 2:2a. "The course of this world" translates *ton aiona tou*

44

kosmou toutou, which may be rendered literally this worldly age. *Kosmou,* "world," is a genitive form and therefore tells us of the kind of an age which is under discussion. Paul wrote from a Roman prison, imprisoned by an emperor unfriendly to the Church of Christ. And we live in an age of worldliness.

> "Is this vile world a friend to grace
> To help us on to God?"

Prof. Sorokin of Harvard declares in *The Crisis of Our Age* that for the past four hundred years the western world has been descending from a civilization spiritually centered to one wholly sensate in which everything is judged by the senses and that we have now arrived at a stage of utter rottenness, reflected in art, music, literature, law, and morals. What an indictment against the period following the renaissance in literature and the reformation in religion! Can this be true? The fact that tremendous powers and boundless resources are devoted to the business of destruction for the second time in our generation persuades us that something is woefully wrong with the world order.

Our text tells us that to walk "according to the course of this world" is to be "dead in trespasses and sins." "Trespasses" translates *paraptomasin,* whose root idea is to fall. Philo said that we had been "Lifted to the heights of heaven but have fallen." The word portrays our stumbling and falling as we travel the journey of life. In classical Greek *paraptoma* signified a blunder. Present day military critics point out how Hitler blundered when he failed to invade England after Dunkirk and his stupid blunder of underestimating the fighting strength of Russia. Men of great responsibility make great blunders, but all men have deviated from the path of rectitude and have parted company with God.

"Sins" translates *hamartiais;* the verb form of which means, to miss. Though the figure changes, yet the force is not different

from that of "trespasses." If one comes to a crossroad and takes
the wrong road it is a case of "missing"; if one attempts to com-
pose a poem on a prosaic subject he has "missed," *hamartano,*
and, in that sense, sinned; if one aims at a bull's eye and hits at
the side of it, he has "missed the mark," *hamartano,* sinned. So
if through worldly influences we have deviated from the high
way of holiness and taken the low road that leads to the valley
of destruction we have sinned. As Trench says of such living,
it is "failing and missing the true scope of our lives which is God."

Such was the sin of Lot and his family in wicked Sodom, of
Solomon led astray by his heathen wives, and of Israel because
she intermarried with heathen nations. Beware, therefore and
"Be not conformed to this world (age, Gr. *aioni*)" (Rom. 12:2);
remember James' warning against world friendship (James 4:4),
and John's admonition to "Love not the world (Gr. *ton kosmon,*
the present world *order*)" (I John 2:15).

But we have been worldly. Yet the power that was sufficient
to raise Christ from the dead has lifted us out of and above the
world so that in God's purpose and by His might we may keep
ourselves "unspotted from the world" (James 1:27).

b. SEPARATED BY THE DEVIL.

We are also separated from God by the devil, our particular
adversary. In Ephesians 2:2 he is said to be, "The prince of the
power of the air, the spirit that now worketh in the children of
disobedience." When we lived in sin we "walked according to"
Satan! *Kata,* rendered "according to," meaning downwards, comes
to signify moving or looking downwards on a thing so as to take
it as a pattern to which we conform. Hence it means according
to Liddell and Scott, agreeable or answering to. How shocking
is the suggestion of this! We once patterned after Satan. Is he
not "The God of this age"? Hath he not "blinded the minds of

them which believe not" (II Cor. 4:4) ? How else can we account for the diabolical conduct of some men—their cruelties and crimes too unspeakably wicked for the ingenuity of even a depraved human?

c. Separated by the Flesh.

And we lived "in times past in the lusts of our flesh" (2:3). Observe that our past lives were "according to" the world and "according to" . . . "the spirit that now worketh in the children of disobedience" but "in the lusts of our flesh." We lived "in" fleshly desires and were dominated by them. The Greek word translated, "lusts," is *epithymiais,* composed of *epi,* upon and *thymos,* desire. *Thymos* is from the verb *thyo,* to rush along and hence to be heated. This term pictures the burning desire of human nature. And "flesh," *sarx,* has for its theological definition mere human nature. To the humanist in religion there is no need of God. Mere human nature is equal to the task of lifting itself by its own bootstraps. But to us who believe in the miracle-working God and the inadequacy of our own powers and propensities to realize His ideal for us, there is no depending upon our own self-effort either for salvation or sanctification.

So the sum total of 2:1-3 is that we "were dead in . . . sins" in that the world, the devil, and the flesh had separated us from God. Environment, the strongest personality apart from God, and our own inherent and inherited nature have conspired to drive us farther and farther from God.

2. BUT GOD INTERVENED (2:4)

"But God, who is rich in mercy, for his great love wherewith he loved us . . . quickened us." How wonderful! "Dead" . . . "quickened!" This is a miracle. Christ's physical body was raised from the dead and so we celebrate Easter Sunday in the church.

And every spiritual birthday is an occasion to commemorate a resurrection of the soul. Oh, the "exceeding greatness of His power!" "But God!" Except for Him we would still be dead in our sins. In mercy He is rich. He pities fallen humanity. And this attitude toward man prompts Him to act on our behalf. Says Trench, "Mercy (*eleos*) has special and immediate regard to the misery which is the consequence of sins." Hence Bengel well said, "Grace takes away blame; mercy, misery."

We observe that this divine intervention arose out of both God's mercy and His love. "Love," *agape,* is His unselfish concern for our good. He loved us "on account of His plenteous love" as the Greek *dio ten pollen agapen autou* indicates. His loving nature motivated Him to do something for us as did the father of the prodigal according to Luke 15:11-32. Pity alone would never have robed and reinstated the returned vagabond. But the father's gifts clothed, fed, and feasted him. And as John 3:16 states, God's love prompted the gift of His Son as a sufficient Saviour for every son of Adam.

3. WE WERE MADE ALIVE AND THUS BROUGHT TO GOD BY GRACE (2:5-8)

We shall consider this as potentially alive (2:5), purposefully raised up (2:6,7), and actually saved (2:8).

"Even us being dead in trespasses he made alive with Christ." So goes the literal rendering of 2:5. *Ontas,* "being," may be a concessive participle. Hence the meaning is that even though we were actually dead yet God had made us alive with Christ. And "with" (Greek *syn*) implies the closest association possible. When He arose from the dead we arose with Him potentially. Hence Colossians 3:1 exhorts us with the words, "If ye then be risen with Christ (therefore since ye were raised up with Christ), seek those things which are above," etc. So Annie Johnson Flint wrote, "Let us go on":

> "Some of us stay at the cross,
> Some of us wait at the tomb,
> Quickened and raised together with Christ,
> Yet lingering still in its gloom.

> "Let us go on with our Lord
> To the fulness of God He has bought,
> Unsearchable riches of glory and good
> Exceeding our uttermost thought."

There is healing in the fountain, but only those who plunge in receive the benefits. In Christ we have an inexhaustible store, but only those who apply and appropriate partake. With native wisdom an old negro settled the matter of the rather difficult doctrine of "election" by declaring that he never did see one elected who was not a candidate. Seeing that God has so abundantly provided for us in Christ how could we refuse His gift of life eternal which is in Christ?

That being "quickened" is synomomous with being "saved" we observe by the introduction of "by grace are ye saved." And our physical, moral, and spiritual resurrection in Christ is followed by our ascension and session with Him. God "caused us to sit down with," *synkathisen,* Christ. And this session is pictured as being *en tois epouraniois,* in the heavenly regions, where God administers. What dignity and dominion does this sitting with Christ above the starry dome of the sky confer upon us! Surely this point of doctrine should make for lofty living. Only royalty sits in the presence of royalty. And our sitting with Christ in the heavens is in line with our "royal priesthood."

But why are we thus exalted? Not for our own glory, but to demonstrate His boundless grace. Other periods of time follow this one. Then we shall show forth "the exceeding riches of His grace." "Exceeding" translates *hyperballon*, which literally means to throw over. On a block of sandstone found in Olympia was the inscription, "Bybon, son of Phorys, with one hand threw me over, *hyperebaleto*, his head." Moulton and Milligan also cite instances where the word meant "outbid" in an auction. So God will show that His grace has riches that go beyond all else in value. He has outbidden every competitor "in His kindness toward us through Christ Jesus." "Kindness," *Chrestoteti*, is graciousness. Trench quotes Tertullian as having said that *"Chrestotes* was so predominantly the character of Christ's ministry that the heathen said 'Christus' became 'Chrestos' and 'Christiani' Chrestiani." And these heathen uttered this in contempt since they did not appreciate the virtues that had the harmlessness of the dove. This same word is derived from the verb *chraomai*, to use. And certainly this quality of "kindness" is most useful to us who deserve harsher measures than God's grace brings.

> "Of grace divine, so wonderful,
> The half was never told."

In order to further magnify the grace of God, Paul tells us just how we have been and are saved; for such is the meaning of "are ye saved," *este sesosmenoi*. Here we have a periphrastic form of the perfect tense which stresses the fact of our having been saved in the past and continuing to be saved in the present. And this is accomplished "By grace," *tei charti*. God's love makes Him merciful (2:4). Therefore He made us alive, raised us up, and seated us in the heavenlies (2:5,6). All this comes to us as the grace of God. It is a satisfying portion as "grace," *charis* basically means. F. W. Farrar, fellow of Trinity College, Cambridge, observes that "grace" occurs thirteen times in the epistle and, he adds, "may be regarded as the most prominent conception of the epistle."

And to explain to us the human as well as the divine part in salvation, the Spirit of God adds "through faith." "For by grace are ye saved through faith" (2:8). The intermediate appropriating agency in salvation is faith, *dia pisteos.* The fourth chapter of Romans is devoted to proving that Abraham was justified by faith apart from works. As verse 16 of that chapter declares, "Therefore it is of faith, that it might be by grace." And the far-reaching effects of appropriating faith are felt as we read in Romans 5:1, "Therefore being justified by faith, we have peace with God through our Lord Jesus Christ." We all realize that God justifies. Yet only they that believe stand before God as justified, declared righteous. As Romans 1:17 says, "The just shall live by faith."

The relation of faith to God's grace in the saving of the soul may be understood by considering the force of the preposition *dia* with the genitive case. In John 1:3 referring to Christ, "The Word," we read, "All things were made by him." In the Greek this is *Panta dia antou egeneto;* literally, all things through Him became. Commenting on this passage Dana and Mantey[1] say, "Although *dia* is occasionally used to express agency, it does not approximate the full strength of *hypo.* This distinction throws light on Jesus' relation to the creation, implying that Jesus was not the absolute independent Creator, but rather the intermediate agent in creation." Since the expression, "through faith," *dia pisteos,* serves the same purpose in "For by grace are ye saved through faith" as that of "through him" in "All things were made through him," we can easily see that faith is the intermediate agency in salvation. And as such it is essential to salvation, "We are . . . of them that believe to the saving of the soul" (Heb. 10:39). "For with the heart man believeth unto righteousness" (Rom. 10:10a).

[1] H. E. Dana and Julius R. Mantey, *Manual Grammar of the Greek N.T.* (MacMillan, N. Y., 1927).

But while discussing faith as so important in salvation there is a danger of our forgetting the divine side, God's "grace"; therefore, inspiration hastens to add, "and that not of yourselves: it is the gift of God." Quite an array of scholars including Chrysostom, Bengel, and Moule maintain that the *touto* in Greek translated "that" refers to "faith"; as though faith is not of ourselves. But the Expositor's Greek Testament states, "But on the other hand the salvation is the main idea in the preceding statement, and it seems best to understand the *kai touto,*" and that, "as referring to that salvation in its entire compass, and not merely to one element in it, its instrumental cause, appended by way of explanation." Yes, salvation is God's gift, *theou to doron.* Christ's death on the cross followed by His resurrection purchased our redemption. Referring to Jesus, Romans 4:25 says, "Who was delivered for our offences, and was raised again for our justification." So salvation is God's gift but only believers appropriate this precious present.

4. OUR WORKS ARE INADEQUATE TO SAVE US (2:9, 10)

a. Otherwise We Might Boast of Saving Ourselves (2:9).

Some decades ago Begbie wrote as foot-notes to Wm. James' "Varieties of Religious Experience" an interesting and illuminating work entitled, "Twice Born Men."[2] In this work Begbie related the life stories of notorious characters of the slums of London who had been transformed by the grace of God. "The Cat Eater," "A Tight Handful," "Old Born Drunk," "The Lowest of the Low," these and numerous others of their kind had knelt in the Salvation Army Hall "consciously unhappy, inferior, and wrong"; and they had been transformed, "saved," by God's

[2] Harold Begbie, *Twice Born Men,* (Fleming H. Revell, N. Y., 1909).

grace and gone out to live lives of lily-white purity. The erstwhile drunkard could not be tempted to drink even though liquor was thrown in his face. Robes once defiled had been washed in the blood of the Lamb.

After citing a sufficient number of these remarkable cases, Begbie says that the psychologists might attempt to explain how all this happened but that no psychologist could produce a single transformation such as these.

Man may reform but he cannot transform. Hence all true soul winners are humble because they are honest. The spirit of self-sufficiency does not characterize the true Christian. He prizes the sacrificial atoning work of Christ on the cross. He looks upon Christ not as an unwilling martyr but as the Son of God willingly suffering the most agonizing, shameful death in order to redeem us from sin. The son of a preacher came to the school of which I was formerly dean of the faculty, to offer for sale what had been the library of his father. These volumes were disposed of at ridiculously low prices. Stevens and Burton's "Harmony of the Gospels" went for a quarter. Why not? The former evangelical preacher had no longer room on the shelves of his library for a volume that showed that Matthew and Luke devoted approximately one-fourth, Mark about one-third, and John nearly one-half of their space to relating the events of the last week of Jesus' life, the climax of which was His death, resurrection, and ascension. Sad indeed had been the declension of this man from the evangelical faith through unitarianism to humanism. And as a humanist he was independent of divine intervention. He thought he could lift himself. What boasting!

b. We Are Only Creatures (2:10a).

"For we are his workmanship." The Greek has it His *poiema*, from *poieo*, to make or do. Let us ever remember that God is the first great cause of all things and we are His product. This term is found in Romans 1:20 where it is translated "the things that are made." From this word we get *poem,* a result of one of the fine arts. And God is the Great Artist and His choicest earthly work is man.

The Psalmist declares, "The heavens declare the glory of God; and the firmament sheweth his handiwork" (Psa. 19:1). Referring to man, "the sweet psalmist of Israel" wrote, "For thou hast made him a little lower than the angels, and hast crowned him with glory and honour" (Psa. 8:5). In expressing this truth David is exalting the Lord, the Creator rather than man the creature, for the psalm both begins and ends with, "O Lord our Lord, how excellent is thy name in all the earth!"

But Lange, with his exegetical accuracy, observes that "created in Christ Jesus" explains in what sense we are God's workmanship. It is as II Corinthians 5:17 states, "If any man be in Christ, he is a new creature." This Christ environment which makes everything different conditions the believer's life. Thus Paul sees the "saved" in this epistle. We are blessed with every spiritual blessing in the heavenlies *in Christ, en Christo* (1:3); He "hath raised us up together, and made us sit together in heavenly places in Christ Jesus, *(en Christo Iesou)"* (2:6); "In the ages to come He might (will) shew the exceeding riches of his grace, in his kindness toward us, through Christ Jesus, *(en Christo Insou)"* (2:7). And in 2:10 we are said to be God's "workmanship" in that we have been "created in Christ Jesus," *en Christo Iesou.*

This mystical union of the believer with Christ is set forth by the Master in the allegory of the vine and the branches of John 15:5. Said He, "I am the vine, ye are the branches: He that abideth in me, and I in him, the same bringeth forth much fruit: for without me ye can do nothing." That being in Christ implies good works as the end or result is clear from the appended phrase "unto good works," *epi ergois agathois.* As verse nine says, our salvation is "not of works," *ouk ex ergon;* salvation is not sourced in works. But after we are saved, works follow as the purpose or consequence of our being new creatures in Christ.

c. GOD PREPARED OUR WORKS BEFORE HE SAVED US (2:10b).

Says Ellicott,[3] *"Before* we were created in Christ, God made ready for us a sphere of moral action, a road, with the intent that we should walk in it and not leave it; this sphere, this road, was good works!" Dean Alford has put it thus, "As trees are created for fruits which God before prepared that they should bear them; i.e., defined and assigned to each tree its own, in form, and flavor, and time of bearing, so in the course of God's providence, our good works are marked out for and assigned to each one of us."

CHAPTER SUMMARY

IN THE HEAVENLIES IN CHRIST (Eph. 2:1-10)

1. We "were dead in trespasses and sins" (vv. 1-3)
   a. Separated by the world (v. 2a).
   b. Separated by the devil (v. 2b).
   c. Separated by the flesh (v. 3).

2. But God Intervened (v. 4)

3. We Were Made Alive and Thus Brought to God by Grace (vv. 5-8)

4. Our Works Are Inadequate to Save Us (vv. 9, 10)
   a. Otherwise we might boast of saving ourselves (v. 9).
   b. We are only creatures (v. 10a).
   c. God prepared our works before He saved us (v. 10b).

---

[3] C. J. Ellicott, *Critical and Grammatical Commentary on Ephesians.* (Draper and Halliday, Boston, 1867).

CHAPTER V

RACIAL RECONCILIATION
(Ephesians 2:11-22)

IN THIS segment of the second chapter of Ephesians, three telling words sum up the whole story. These are "far off," *makran;* "nigh," *engys;* "reconcile," *apokatallaxe.* The first of these terms, *makran,* means *long,* and therefore suggests the distance that separated the Gentiles from God. Now the separation of any people from God is not an arbitrary thing but is due to a principle. Said the Lord to Israel, "But your *iniquities have separated* between you and your God, and your sins have hid his face from you, that he will not hear" (Isa. 59:2). Under the dispensation of law God gave His chosen people a chance to draw near to Him by sacrifices and the keeping of the commandments. In Leviticus 18 we have directions given for proper conduct in view of earthly relationships. Certain sinful practices are forbidden. Then follows the exhortation: "Defile not ye yourselves in any of these things: for in all these the nations are defiled which I cast out before you: And the land is defiled: therefore I do visit the iniquity thereof upon it, and the land itself vomiteth out her inhabitants" (Lev. 18:24, 25). Canaan had become nauseated through revolting filthy sexual sins. Hence the Canaanites were spued out.

There are those who look upon the expulsion of the Canaanites by Israel as "savagery." But as Dr. Earl Pierce says,[1] it is the *savagery of surgery.* In order to save the life of the patient the

---

[1] Earl Pierce, *The Church and World Conditions.*

surgeon must mutilate the body, cut into good tissue and shed good blood. But the end requires and justifies the means. Health necessitates the ridding of the patient of the malignant growth. Just so sin makes it imperative that the sinner be "far" from God.

1. THE GENTILES WERE "FAR OFF" (2:11, 12)

a. UNCIRCUMCISION (2:11).

Among the Israelites uncircumcision was a term of reproach. David disdaining Goliath, the champion of the enemy, referred to him twice as "this uncircumcised Philistine" (I Sam. 17:26, 36). We observe that the Gentiles "are called Uncircumcision by that which is called Circumcision." Here is a hint as to how Paul had come to regard circumcision. In Philippians 3:2, 3 he refers to it as the "concision," *katatome,* a cutting up or mutilation and states that "we are the circumcision." So he does not allow any true religious significance to circumcision as practiced by the Jews but claims a spiritual circumcision for true Christians, who before conversion were "far off" from God but now are partakers of the new covenant. A further belittling epithet is added in "made by hands," *cheiropoietou,* literally, hand made or "manufactured."

b. APART FROM CHRIST (2:12).

"Without" translates *choris,* a word connected with *chora,* a tract of land or space between two limits. When we think of the significance of the believer being in Christ, *en Christo,* as Ephesians sets forth, we can appreciate the meaning of being separated from Him. As prodigals we were in "a far country."

c. ALIENATED FROM THE COMMONWEALTH OF ISRAEL (2:12).

"Aliens" is from the Greek *allotrios,* belonging to another; hence "foreign." Since the promises and the covenants were to the advantage of Israel only, we Gentiles were without heavenly citizenship until Jesus took us in.

d. "STRANGERS FROM THE COVENANTS OF PROMISE" (2:12).

"Strangers," *Xenoi,* is a word that refers either to the hosts or the guests. It brings the picture of the oriental or bedouin receiving a stranger into his tent. They are unknown or foreigners to each other. And the provisions and promises of God's covenants were unknown to us before we were accepted by God the Father in the Son. In the covenant with Abraham (Gen. 12:2, 3) the Lord said, "And in thee shall all families of the earth be blessed." This included us but its fulfillment was not realized by us until we took Christ as our Saviour.

e. "HAVING NO HOPE" (2:12).

"So long as there is life there is hope," is a proverb the very recital of which reminds us of how utterly forlorn are those who have lost hope. Hope implies some expectation. Referring to world conditions before Christ came a modern writer has said, "For thousands of years, the common people of the earth had lived without hope of anything better than drudgery, slavery, and starvation. Always the rapacious rulers of some empire were murdering and pillaging the helpless." Into such a world dominated by ruthless Rome, Christ came saying, "Ye shall know the truth, and the truth shall make you free" (John 8:32). "The law was given by Moses, but grace and truth came by Jesus Christ" (John 1:17). "The law made nothing perfect, but the bringing in of a better hope did; by the which we draw nigh unto God" (Heb. 7:19). "Which hope we have as an anchor of the soul, both sure and stedfast, and which entereth into that within the veil; Whither the forerunner is for us entered, even Jesus" (Heb. 6:19, 20).

So that with jubilation the Christian may now sing:

> "My hope is built on nothing less
> Than Jesus' blood and righteousness.
> I dare not trust the sweetest frame,
> But wholly lean on Jesus' name.
> On Christ the solid Rock I stand,
> All other ground is sinking sand."

f. "WITHOUT GOD IN THE WORLD" (2:12).

Atheoi from which we get *atheism* is the Greek word rendered, "Without God." Literally, the word means *not god* or *gods;* so to be *atheoi* is to recognize and worship no God. Lange's commentary[2] recognizes three senses in which the expression may be used: *active* (opposed to God), *neuter* (ignorant of God) and *passive* (forsaken of God). He believes with Hodge, Eadie, Ellicott, and Alford that the passive sense is intended here since the whole passage is passive. Since God is "the God of hope" to be without hope is to be without God.

Observe that the text speaks of being "without God in the world." By "world" is meant the world as we think of its harmony and arrangement. Our earthly sphere rotates on its axis with regularity. It stays in its prescribed orbit without deviation. The seasons come and go as planned by the Creator. Seeds germinate and in orderly succession we have the stock, the blade, the ear, and the full corn in the ear. Birds and beasts and creeping things behave according to their natures as altered by the Fall, but man is unpredictable except in his certainty to miss the mark which God originally set for him. "All have sinned, and come short of the glory of God" (Rom. 3:23). To be without God in a world hopelessly confused by the wickedness of man is a plight pathetic beyond description. Who can find his way out of this

---

[2] *Lange's Commentary on Ephesians.* Translation and additions by M. B. Riddle, D.D. (Chas. Scribner's Sons, N. Y., 1879).

wilderness of woe without God to guide? We are lost in the darkness and need the Light of God—according to Tennyson:

> "Children crying in the night,
> Children crying for the light
> And with no language but a cry!"

Ancient Egypt could temper copper and could adjust the gigantic stones of the pyramids to a mathematical line and not vary a hair's breadth; and yet she came to decay because she worshipped the calf, the creature, rather than God the Creator. Men "changed the glory of the uncorruptible God into an image made like to corruptible man, and to birds, and fourfooted beasts, and creeping things. Wherefore God also gave them up to uncleanness" (Rom. 1:23, 24). O, the tragedy of being "given up" by God. An officer "gives over" a prisoner to be incarcerated and thus separated from society. And our God, who loves us, because of our sinful condition must surrender us to our sinful state unless we receive cleansing through the blood of Christ.

2. THE JEWS AND THE GENTILES WHO ARE "IN CHRIST" HAVE BECOME "NIGH" (2:13-15a)

a. "By the Blood of Christ" (2:13).

Verse thirteen begins with "But now, in Christ Jesus." "Now" translates *nyni* which is emphatic as over against the usual, *nyn*. We might say, "now at this very minute" or we, in speaking, might utter, "now," with force. The word is in contrast with "sometimes," *pote,* aforetime. Things are different with us since Christ died, rose, and ascended to the Father. We may come boldly to the throne of grace as says the author of Hebrews.

Leviticus 10:1, 2 relates the sad story of Nadab and Abihu, sons of Aaron, the high priest, offering strange fire to God and being destroyed with fire from God. Their "strange fire" did not bring them "nigh" to God. And, as Leviticus 16 records, after this incident, the Lord instructed Moses as to how Aaron might make atonement once a year for himself and the people. This was to be done with blood. Great care was to be taken to carry out God's plan that Aaron "die not." Commenting on this Hebrews 9:11-14 says, "But Christ being come an high priest of good things to come, by a greater and more perfect tabernacle, not made with hands, that is to say, not of this building; neither by the blood of goats and calves, but by his own blood he entered in once into the holy place, having obtained eternal redemption for us. For if the blood of bulls and of goats, and the ashes of an heifer sprinkling the unclean, sanctifieth to the purifying of the flesh; how much more shall the blood of Christ, who through the eternal Spirit offered himself without spot to God, purge your conscience from dead works to serve the living God?" And since, "Without shedding of blood is no remission" (Heb. 9:22), the converse is true and the shedding of blood brings remission of sin. But it is His blood that avails.

> "Not all the blood of beasts
> On Jewish altars slain,
> Could give the guilty conscience peace,
> Or wash away the stain:
>
> But Christ, the heavenly Lamb,
> Takes all our sins away;
> A sacrifice of nobler name,
> And richer blood than they."
> —Isaac Watts

"Having, therefore, brethren boldness to enter into the holiest by the blood of Jesus . . . Let us draw near with a true heart in full assurance of faith" (Heb. 10:19, 22).

b. In Christ We Find the Basis of Peace (2:14a).

When Jesus left Nazareth to dwell in Capernaum where so many Gentiles resided, Matthew saw the fulfillment of the prophecy of Isaiah (9:1-6), "The land of Zabulon, and the land of Nephthalim, by the way of the sea, beyond Jordan, Galilee of the Gentiles; The people which sat in darkness saw a great light" (Matt. 4:15, 16). So Jesus was letting His light shine on Jew and Gentile alike. As Isaiah continues, "His name shall be called Wonderful, Counselor, The mighty God, The everlasting Father, The Prince of Peace." He was the leader of peace. Upon the birth of Christ the multitude of heavenly host with the angel which spoke to the shepherds said, "Glory to God in the highest, and on earth peace, good will toward men" (Luke 2:14). Among the beatitudes of Jesus we find, "Blessed are the peacemakers: for they shall be called the children of God" (Matt. 5:9).

Henry Clay is known in American history as "The Great Pacificator" because he attempted to keep the peace by the method of compromise, "give and take." But Christ, Himself, *autos,* as the Greek has it, is our peace. He "made both one." He does this by indwelling the believer and thus reigns within and prompts us to "Endeavor to keep the unity of the Spirit in the bond of peace" as we shall study in chapter four.

In a day when race problems are unsolved, when "the leading negro Christian College President in America," Mordecai W. Johnson, of Howard University, foresees a possible war in which the darker people would "be pitted against the United States in a fight to the finish," when the Jews are subjected to persecutions, pogroms and deportations, in such a day of hatred and strife, of war and carnage culminating in most heated antipathy among the sons of Adam, we do well to remember, "For he is our peace who hath made both one."

c. CHRIST RENDERED INOPERATIVE THE LAW THAT SEPARATED
    (2:14b, 15a).

In showing that the believer is not made holy by the law, Paul says in its justification, "The law is holy, and the commandment holy, and just, and good" (Rom. 7:12). What stronger statement could be made in favor of any code or instrument? In explaining how the believer is saved by faith apart from the works of the law, Paul sets forth just why the law came into existence and what useful purpose it served. Wrote he in Galatians 3:19 and 24, "It was added because of transgressions, till the seed should come to whom the promise was made. . . ." "The law was our schoolmaster (pedagogue) to bring us unto Christ, that we might be justified by faith." The law said, do this but do not do that. And the law brought us to Him who said, "Think not that I am come to destroy the law, or the prophets: I am not come to destroy, but to fulfill" (Matt. 5:17). And fulfill it He did, for of Him the Father said, "This is my beloved Son, in whom I am well pleased" (Matt. 3:17; 17:5b). He was "the seed of the woman," Abraham's seed, to whom the promise was made.

Observe the three words used in 2:15, "law . . . commandments . . . ordinances." The "law," *nomos,* included all the civil, ceremonial, moral, and sanitary directions for the conduct of God's people. This law, given through Moses, was stated in the form of commandments, *entolai,* injunctions served upon the people. And these "commandments" were in the nature of "ordinances," *dogmata,* decrees. Of this expression Thayer gives as a rendering "the law containing precepts in the form of decrees." Such forceful "ordinances," *dogmata,* were the pronouncements of the ruthless, absolute Roman emperors as Luke 2:1 states. But however forceful, binding and explicit these laws were Jesus "abolished" them "in His flesh." The Greek word *katargesas* translated "abolished" is composed of *kata* plus *a* (meaning not) and *ergon* (work). Hence the word has as its root meaning to cause not to work. Just as slavery was "abolished" or rendered inoperative in the United States by the emancipation proclamation, enforced by the victories of the Federal Arms, so the law that bound

Israel to a legal life was abolished by the death of Christ which climaxed a perfect life.

3. CHRIST RECONCILED BOTH JEW AND GENTILE TO GOD (2:15b-22)

"Reconcile" translates *apokatallaxe,* a compound word made up of *apo,* back, *kata* and *allasso,* change. Hence it signifies to change back to a former condition. In discussing 2:1 we observed that sin had separated man from God. Then we note the distinction between Jew and Gentile in the economy of God as set forth in 2:11. The word "reconcile" implies not only a bringing back into fellowship with God both Jew and Gentile but also that these are brought together as children of Adam, the federal head of the human race. In Christ there is no Jew; there is no Gentile. All are of a kind. How different are human relations when this is realized.

a. THROUGH HIM, JEW AND GENTILE BECOME A NEW TYPE OF MAN (2:15b).

The purpose of Christ's abolishing the enmity which existed between Jew and Gentile due to different attitudes toward "the law of commandments contained in ordinances" was "to make in Himself of twain one new man, so making peace." Christ suffered the penalty of a broken law; He fulfilled the requirements of the commandments to bring in a new era of peace and good will among men. So Christ's death was creative as "make," *ktisei,* really means. He created "one new man." "New," *kainon,* in the sense of a new kind of a man, rather than a recent man. The Christian is a new type. And so he is expected to be. His ethical system is the highest. Of the spurious Christian alone is the word "hypocrite" used. The doctrines of the early Christian church were so other-worldly as to "turn the world upside down."

Humility, kindness, charity, and repentance came into their own as embodied in the Christian. Hence the possibility of peace.

b. Jew and Gentile Are Now "in One Body" (2:16).

The phrase "in one body" evidently tells us of the sphere of our reconciliation. Christ "reconciled both unto God in one body." Where there were two now there is one in Christ. This interpretation of 2:16 is shared by Hodge, Alford, and Ellicott according to Lange.[8] As Paul says in I Corinthians 12:12, "For as the body is one, and hath many members, and all the members of that one body, being many, are one body: so also is Christ." Here the mystical body of Christ is referred to. It is made up of all regenerate believers whether they be Jew or Gentile. So a "Jewish Christian" is no more or less than a Christian just as is a Gentile Christian. This has been done "by the Cross." Here the Greek has *dia ton staurou,* through the Cross. What was an instrument of torture and a symbol of shame became the intermediate implement of salvation, reconciliation, and peace. Glorious substitutionary suffering of our Saviour!

c. Jew and Gentile Heard the Good News of Peace Through Christ (2:17).

When Christ died Israel was under the galling yoke of Rome. Pilate, representative of the Gentile power, pressed by the Jewish leaders, had Christ crucified. By His death Jesus spoke more clearly to Jew and Gentile than He ever did by life and word. When Nicodemus, "the teacher of Israel" (Greek of John 3:10), came to Jesus by night, the Master finally said to him, "And as Moses lifted up the serpent in the wilderness, even so must the Son of man be lifted up: That whosoever believeth in him should not perish, but have eternal life" (John 3:14, 15). When certain worshipping Greeks said to Philip, "Sir, we would see Jesus" and

---

[8] *Ibid.*

when Andrew and Philip had transmitted this message to Jesus, He said: "Verily, verily, I say unto you, Except a corn of wheat fall into the ground and die it abideth alone: but if it die, it bringeth forth much fruit . . . Now is my soul troubled; and what shall I say? Father, save me from this hour: but for this cause came I unto this hour" (John 12:21, 24, 27). Jesus was born that He might die. Death to Him was not an accident nor tragedy but a glorious consummation of His life. He tasted death for every man (Heb. 2:9), and "ye are all the children of God by faith in Christ Jesus. For as many of you as have been baptized into Christ have put on Christ. There is neither Jew nor Greek, there is neither bond nor free, there is neither male nor female: for ye are all one in Christ Jesus. And if ye be Christ's, then are ye Abraham's seed, and heirs according to the promise" (Gal. 3:26-29). In the presence of the cross of Christ, man made human barriers are removed. All are joint heirs. All hear His beautiful bequest of peace: "Peace I leave with you, my peace I give unto you: not as the world giveth, give I unto you" (John 14:27).

d. They Both Have An Approach to God (2:18).

"For through him we both have access by one Spirit unto the Father" is a statement which includes the whole trinity. The heart of true religion is God-consciousness. Said a great thinker, "Religion is living in time for eternity under the eye and with the help of God." "Through Him," *dia antou,* as the intermediate Agent, we both, (hand in hand) have access . . . "unto the Father." Since Christ is our great high priest, "Let us therefore come boldly unto the throne of grace" (Heb. 4:16). And we have access in one Spirit, *en heni pneumati.* It is in the fellowship of the Holy Spirit that we come. As Lange[4] says, the prepositions are well chosen; we come unto the Father through Christ in the Spirit.

[4] *Ibid.*

e. They Constitute One "Household" (2:19).

Here we see teaching by contrast. We are not "strangers," *xenoi,* unknown to one another, but "fellowcitizens," *synpolitai,* living in the same city; we are not "foreigners," *paroikoi,* residing elsewhere, but "of the household of God," *oikeioi* which has as its meaning intimately associated, of the same family and blood. Much misunderstanding comes from ignorance of one another. Companionship implies eating bread together. In Christ we have a common "love feast," a "communion."

f. Christ is the Standard of Jew and Gentile (2:20).

In this verse Christians are seen as "living stones" (I Pet. 2:5), comprising the superstructure of the church. The apostles and prophets were active in the laying of the foundation of this building. But what they were as builders and building material was in keeping with Christ who is the "chief corner stone," *akrogonaiou.* Of this word Moulton and Milligan[5] quote W. W. Lloyd as saying, "The *akrogonaios* (chief cornerstone) here is the primary foundation-stone at the angle of the structure by which the architect fixes a standard for the bearings of the walls and cross walls throughout." Recall Peter's confession, "Thou art the Christ, the Son of the living God" (Matt. 16:16) and our Lord's statement to him: "Thou art Peter *(petros),* and upon this rock, (petra) I will build my church" (Matt. 16:18). "Rock" as used here is *petra,* a large stone, whereas "Peter," *petros,* according to Schmidt, is a detached fragment of stone. Certainly Peter was of the Rock, Christ Jesus. All that Peter the apostle was and did emanated from "the Christ the Son of the Living God." And upon the tremendous fact of Jesus being the Son of God the church was built. So just as Christ as the "chief corner stone" determined the entire building work as well as the character of

---

[5] Moulton and Milligan. *Vocabulary of the Greek N.T.* (Hodder and Stoughton, London, 1930). One volume edition.

the apostles and prophets, including Peter, so He determines us as to what we are and do. The Christian should be Christlike regardless of race, color, or creed. Upon considering any new task or venture his first question should always be "What would Jesus do?"

g. "In Christ Jesus" Gentile and Jew Comprise a "Holy Temple" Indwelt by the Spirit of God (2:21, 22).

The intimacy of the union of the various members of the body of Christ, the Church, is expressed by "fitly framed together." Carrying on the figure of a building we recall how each tenon fits snugly into a mortise prepared according to accurate measurement in order to have a strong structure. The Greek word used here is *synarmologoumene,* composed of *syn,* together, *armos,* a joint, and *lego* to lay or place. Hence the word describes the joining of the members of the body together. Thus are we associated in Christ.

"Ye also are builded together for an habitation of God through the Spirit" is a sacred and solemnizing utterance. When God had appeared to Jacob in a dream the latter said: "Surely the Lord is in this place; and I knew it not. And he was afraid, and said, How dreadful is this place! This is none other but the house of God, and this is the gate of heaven . . . and he called the name of that place Bethel" (Gen. 28:16-19). God, speaking to Moses from the burning but unconsumed bush, demanded, "Draw not nigh hither: put off thy shoes from off thy feet, for the place whereon thou standest is holy ground" (Exod. 3:5). Into the Holy of holies of the temple sanctuary, the High Priest alone was permitted to enter and that only once a year after he had made special preparation (Lev. 16:1-34). David asks, "Lord, who shall abide in thy tabernacle? who shall dwell in thy holy hill?" The answer includes the highest ethical if not religious requirements (Psa. 15:1-5).

Considering these Old Testament scriptures, it seems all the more wonderful that we are "an habitation of God." And "temple" translates the Greek *naon,* "used of the temple at Jerusalem, but only the sacred edifice (or sanctuary) itself, consisting of the Holy place and the Holy of holies" (Thayer). So as God was manifest in the Holy of holies so is He evidently present in His church. And observe that the temple mentioned here is described as "holy," *hagion,* set apart for sacred uses. And so we "in Christ," Gentile and Jew alike, are devoted to the sacred service of being God's dwelling place. "If any man have not the Spirit of Christ, he is none of his" (Rom. 8:9). Thus the indwelling Spirit characterizes every true believer.

CHAPTER SUMMARY

RACIAL RECONCILIATION (Eph. 2:11-22)

1. The Gentiles Were "Far Off" (vv. 11,12)
   a. Uncircumcision (v. 11).
   b. Apart from Christ (v. 12a).
   c. Alienated from the commonwealth of Israel (v. 12b).
   d. "Strangers from the covenants of promise" (v. 12c).
   e. "Having no hope" (v. 12d).
   f. "Without God in the world" (v. 12e).
2. The Jews and the Gentiles Who Are in Christ Have Become "Nigh" (vv. 13-15a)
   a. "By the blood of Christ" (v. 13).
   b. In Christ we find the basis of peace (v. 14a).
   c. Christ rendered inoperative the law that separated (v. 14b, 15a).
3. Christ Reconciled Both Jew and Gentile to God (vv. 15b-22)
   a. Through Him Jew and Gentile become a new type of man (v. 15b).
   b. Jew and Gentile are now "in one body" (v. 16).
   c. Jew and Gentile heard the good news of peace through Christ (v. 17).
   d. They both have an approach to God (v. 18).
   e. They constitute one "household" (v. 19).
   f. Christ is the standard of Jew and Gentile (v. 20).
   g. "In Christ Jesus" Gentile and Jew comprise a "holy temple" indwelt by the Spirit of God (vv. 21, 22).

Chapter VI

THE DISPENSATION OF THE GRACE OF GOD
(Ephesians 3:1-12)

IN THE vocabulary of the church we speak of a "dispensation" when we mean a period of time in which God deals in a particular way with mankind in respect to sin and man's responsibility to him. During the dispensation of law, which extended from the giving of the law on Mount Sinai through Moses until Christ died on the cross of Calvary, Israel was held responsible to obey the precepts of the law. To disobey was to sin and to be punished accordingly.

But here we deal with "the dispensation of the grace of God." The Greek term is *oikonormia,* literally the law or rule of a house. It refers to a particular plan or arrangement and then the management or execution of that plan. The particular plan under view here is that which is characterized by God's grace. "The law was given through Moses; grace and truth came through Jesus Christ" (John 1:17 R.V.). So "the dispensation of the grace of God" is the Christian dispensation.

We note further that this arrangement in the divine economy was "given me to you-ward" as Paul says to the church. The apostle was the recipient in a special way, and it is for our benefit. Therefore Paul, after showing how we were saved by grace through faith and that both Gentile and Jew are one in Christ, opens this chapter with, "For this cause I Paul, the prisoner of Jesus Christ for you Gentiles." He is not the prisoner of Nero, the Roman Emperor, but of Christ Jesus. Nero, though very self-important, is only an instrument used by Christ Jesus. Nothing comes into the apostle's life except by Christ's permission. And this confinement is "for you Gentiles," *hyper hymon ton ethnon.* "For," *hyper* means for the sake of or instead of. Called to be the apostle to the Gentiles, Paul suffered for their sake. And no such service as his can be rendered without personal inconvenience and some suffering. E. Y. Mullins in "Why Is Christianity True" lauds the altruistic motive of missionaries. He quotes one who said, "The ideal missionary must have four passions: for the truth . . . for Christ . . . for the souls of men and . . for self-sacrifice." Paul was "an ambassador in a chain." Because he gave the gospel to the nations he was imprisoned. And your ministry to others may lead to your inconvenience. Yet we would not have it otherwise. Give us service with suffering if these two must go together. The ambassador of Christ has no selfish "Safety First" for his motto.

The expression, "If ye have heard," in verse two was evidently not intended to indicate that Paul doubted that his readers had heard. He had taught daily in the school of Tyrannus for at least two years. Certainly his message was carried throughout the surrounding region. Technically speaking, the Greek form here is a condition fulfilled. Hence, "since ye have heard" is a fair rendering. Alford and Ellicott have it, "Assuming that ye have heard." So faithful had been the apostolic witness to the great truths of the gospel that he could send this circulatory letter out with confidence as to the reader's readiness to receive it.

1. THE MYSTERY OF THIS DISPENSATION WAS REVEALED TO PAUL FOR US (3:3-5)

"Mystery," *mysterion* in Greek, means that which has been concealed hitherto but is now revealed. And "revelation," *apokalypcis,* is literally an unveiling. As the veil of the temple concealed the holy of holies from the holy place so the veil of secrecy covered the precious truth of the dispensation of grace until God disclosed this to Paul.

And this revelation was not vouchsafed to Paul that he might indulge himself in the luxury of its contents. But rather as he says, "when ye read, ye may understand my knowledge in the mystery of Christ." And since this revelation is found in the Greek language, we may count upon it as being satisfactory and beautiful because, as Dana and Mantey[1] say, the Greek language is most "accurate, euphonious, and expressive."

Observe that this knowledge has to do with "the mystery of Christ." Christ was typified, predicted, and expected according to the Old Testament. He is seen incarnate in the gospel, but the full revelation of all that He is and means to us is revealed in the Epistles and Revelation.

And as the Expositors' Greek Testament points out this especial revelation was not made known to "the sons of men," that is men in general, in other generations, but now it is revealed to "apostles, (*apostolois*, those officially sent by God) and prophets (*prophetois*, those who speak for God) by the Spirit." And these are both said to be "holy," *hagiois*, separated, and devoted to this work of revealing God's plan for us. So important is the divine task of these men that that work overshadows anything else they may do. If Paul makes tents or travels extensively, this is subservient to his apostolic mission. Likewise Peter's fishing must not deter him as a spokesman of God. Let us see to it that our Christian service is always our major task even if it does not occupy the most of our time.

2. THE MEANING OF THIS MYSTERY (3:6)

The "mystery" referred to in verse three is defined in verse six as "That the Gentiles should be fellow-heirs, and of the same

---

[1] Dana and Mantey. *Manual Grammar of the Greek N. T.*

body, and partakers of his promise in Christ by the gospel." To frightened shepherds on the hills of Judea, appeared an angel of the Lord announcing, "Behold, I bring you good tidings of great joy, which shall be *to all people*" (Luke 2:10). Here we have the first mention of "the gospel," *to evangelion,* the evangel, the good news. The substance of these tidings was "There is born to you today a Saviour, who is Christ the Lord." A striking feature of this announcement was that it was "to all the people." Gentiles also receive this good news.

Paul, writing to Timothy, refers "to the church of the living God (as) the pillar and ground of truth," i.e., the support, *stylos,* and seat, *hedraioma,* of truth. Then he gives that truth as being, "God was manifested in the flesh . . . preached unto the Gentiles" (I Tim. 3:15, 16). And he calls this truth, "the mystery of godliness." Hence we see that the prominent thing about this "mystery" is that all men now are supposed to share its meaning. It is no longer "To the Jew first." The Jew has already had the "first" opportunity to accept Christ as his Messiah.

The English text says that the Gentiles are fellow-heirs of the same body and partakers of His promise in Christ by the gospel. The Greek text employs the preposition *syn,* with, three times in rapid succession to impress the unity of all races "in Christ." As my distinguished colleague, Prof. Kenneth Wuest, of Moody Bible Institute, puts it, "Gentile and Jew are amalgamated in one body in Christ." All share alike in the riches of His grace. All are one in Christ. All or any may claim the promises.

3. THE MINISTER OF THIS MYSTERY (3:7-9)

Says Paul, referring still to the mystery, "Of which I became a minister." The term used for "minister" is *diakonos* concerning which Moulton and Milligan say, "A definitely religious connotation belongs to the word . . . the remains of a list of temple

officials concludes with *diakonos.*" And Thieme speaks of a
college of *diakonoi* presided over by a priest. The verb form is
cited by the Oxyrhynchus papyri as translated, "to serve and do
everything commanded him." As to its etymology some think it
comes from *diuko,* I hasten; others maintain it is from *dioko,* I
follow; others claim that it originates from *dia* plus *konos,* dust.
Hence its root meaning may be to follow, as Immanuel Kant's
servant always did, carrying a raincoat and an umbrella lest his
master would get wet when he took his daily stroll on a threatening day. Or its root idea may be to hasten and so raise the
dust as does a diligent servant hurrying about in the doing of his
several duties. "Minister," *diakonos,* is by some said to be the
best word for an ecclesiastical servant.

a. THIS MINISTRY IS A GIFT (3:7).

It was "according to the gift of the grace of God." Noted
though this honored servant of God became, yet he was aware
that his ministry was not "earned" by him but given by God.
And what a gracious, satisfying, gift was Paul. He came "by
the effectual working of God's power." Divine omnipotence,
dynamis, the dynamo of deity, gave to this servant unusual energy,
energeian. And how energetic was he, although "weak" in body,
yet he could preach all night or walk along the shore as the ship
on which he traveled plied the sea.

b. THE HUMILITY OF THE MINISTER (3:8a).

Feeling the poverty of even the Greek language, the writer
styles himself "less than the least of all saints." *Elachistotero* is
literally "leaster." If one is least how can he be less than that?
Yet Paul places a comparative ending on a superlative form. I
once heard Billy Sunday refer to some mean men as being "so

low down that they would have to reach up to scratch bottom."
In the light of his high calling the apostle sees his own insignifi-
cance and sensing the value of the "saints" as a whole he would
demean himself. Since size, sanctity, and qualifications are relative matters should not we who hold forth the torch of truth today
be genuinely humble in the light of the glorious gospel of God's
grace for all men?

This grace of humility is most becoming to the servant of
Christ while its opposite, pride, is pathetic if not detestable. In a
footnote Eadie[2] quotes from Baxter's Works, *The Reformed
Pastor,* on this matter. What he so caustically condemns was true
in 1830. Is it a fair description of pulpit pride today? I quote in
part:

> "Pride is so prevalent in some of us, that it inditeth our
> discourses for us . . . it formeth our countenances, it putteth
> the accents and emphasis upon our words . . . It persuadeth
> us to paint the window that it may dim the light . . . And
> when pride hath made the sermon, it goeth with us into the
> pulpit; it formeth our tones . . . it setteth us in pursuit of
> vain applause. It makes us ask, 'What shall I say and how
> shall I deliver it to be thought a learned, able preacher, and
> to be applauded by all that hear me?' "

But pride is not reflected by the ministry alone. It is related
that Parrhasius, a famous painter, resided in Ephesus. His arro-
gance and conceit were proverbial. He claimed to receive divine
communications. How striking is the contrast between such a
one noted for voluptuous and self-indulgent habits and the apostle
who, though he wrote by inspiration, styles himself "less than the
least of all saints."

---

[2] John Eadie, D.D., LL.D., Commentary on the Greek text of the Epistle of Paul
to the Ephesians. (Clark, 1883). Third Edition.

c. This Ministry is Definite as to Its Scope and Subject (3:8b).

Paul was to "preach among the Gentiles the unsearchable riches of Christ." When Saul of Tarsus was converted the Lord said to Ananias, "He is a chosen vessel unto me, to bear my name before the Gentiles, and kings, and the children of Israel" (Acts 9:15). In writing to the Romans, Paul said, "For I speak to you Gentiles, inasmuch as I am the apostle of the Gentiles, I magnify mine office" (Rom. 11:13).

What transformation God can work! Here is one who had been a Pharisee of the Pharisees, an exclusive Israelite, whose whole attitude was changed. So much so that he specializes in giving the good news of salvation to the non-Jewish nations. Since God can change an aloof, self-righteous Pharisee into a missionary to other peoples, who could have the effrontery to despise the miraculous might of the Almighty?

And what Paul has to give as the ambassador of King Jesus he aptly styles, "the unsearchable riches of Christ." Eadie[3] relates that "Scipio, on the eve of the battle of Pharsalia, had threatened to take possession of the vast sums hoarded up in the temple of Diana, and Mark Anthony had exacted a nine-years' tax in two years' payment; but Paul and his colleagues were declared on high authority not to be robbers of churches." They circulated "riches."

"Unsearchable riches!" What are they? Men have died in quest of riches. Men find earthly riches. But just what are "unsearchable riches." First, we observe that they are "of Christ," *tou Christou.* They are associated with or belong to Christ—Christian riches! Said Paul to the Philippians, "My God shall supply every need of yours according to his riches in glory by Christ Jesus." And "unsearchable," *anexichniaston,* is composed of the verb, *exichniazo* to trace out and *a* which makes the mean-

---

[3] *Ibid.*

ing negative. Hence the "unsearchable" is that which cannot be traced out or comprehended. When we contemplate what Jesus Christ has brought to us, we agree that it is precious beyond our comprehension. Take the matter of salvation from sins. While others than evangelical believers are working and paying with the faint hope of possibly sometime getting out of purgatorial fires, we who accept the Bible for what it actually says rejoice that "By grace are ye saved through faith" and that "He that believeth and is baptized shall be saved." And consider the promise of heaven made by the Master to His disciples: "I go to prepare a place for you. And if I go and prepare a place for you, I will come again, and receive you unto myself; that where I am, there ye may be also." Or ponder the picture of heaven painted in a few bold strokes by Peter: "An inheritance incorruptible, and undefiled, and that fadeth not away, reserved in heaven for you." Unspeakably rich are we; and we are sons of the King of kings.

d. This Ministry is Missionary (3:9a).

Added to the responsibility of preaching among the Gentiles the unsearchable riches of Christ is this: "to make all see what is the fellowship of the mystery." "To make . . . (to) see" is a rendering of *photisai,* to illumine. The term is used repeatedly for spiritual illumination. Hence preaching is not merely passing on information. It is a sublime art. The evangelist must be illuminated in order to be illuminating.

And he is "to make all see." The "church's marching orders" were to go into all the world and to herald the good news to every creature (Mark 16:15). Since the days of William Carey, especially, the Christian Church has been aroused to her responsibility to "evangelize." And missionary churches are growing churches and spiritual fellowships. And, incidentally, we observe here that what all men should see is "the fellowship of the mystery" or the plan of God which includes Jew and Gentile in one body of believers in Christ. When Jews see this they become Christians, and when Gentiles see this they love the Jew and strive for his conversion. Herein is the secret of peace and the solution of the race problem.

e. THIS MYSTERY HAS BEEN HIDDEN HITHERTO IN GOD (3:9b).

We should be grateful for all of God's revelations. Our life is but as a vapor which appeareth for a little time and then vanisheth away. He is from everlasting to everlasting. And, until our dispensation of grace, God chose to conceal his plan for one universal redemption through Christ. "From the beginning of the world hath been hid in God," speaks of the prolonged and profound silence of deity. Literally, this is "from the ages," *apo ton aionon.* Says John Eadie,[4] "Until Jesus' death the means were not provided by which Judaism could be superseded and a world-wide system introduced."

And who may question the propriety of this divine concealment of a truth so unspeakably precious? For was it not "God who created all things by Jesus Christ"? The Creator would know what to reveal and to whom and when to reveal this. As Galatians 4:4 (R.V.) says, "When the fulness of the time came, God sent forth his Son." Before Christ's coming there had been centuries of silence. Heaven had not been speaking to earth. It was as though all creation was in the suspense of awe before the Father said, "This is my beloved Son, in whom I am well pleased." "The Word became flesh, and dwelt among us, and we beheld his glory." "God, who at sundry times and in divers manners spoke to the fathers by the prophets, hath in these last days spoken unto us by his Son." So the "mystery" was hidden, *apo kekrymmenou,* as absolutely as one digs a hole in the earth and conceals a treasure, as did the man with one talent of Matthew

---
[4] *Ibid.*

25:18—this mystery thus concealed for millenniums was revealed in God's good time, "the fulness of time," as verse ten says, "now."

4. THE MANIFESTATION OF THE MYSTERY (3:10)

Some of Paul's sentences are long and involved. Verses 8, 9, 10, 11, and 12 comprise one continued statement. In brief, the thought is that grace was given to Paul to preach the gospel among the Gentiles and to make all men see God's plan in order that the manifold wisdom of God might be caused to be made known to angelic beings.

What is "the manifold wisdom of God"? In I Corinthians 1:23, 24 we read, "We preach Christ crucified, unto the Jews a stumblingblock, and unto the Greeks foolishness; But unto them which are called, both Jews and Greeks, Christ the power of God, and the wisdom of God." Therefore, in Christ we see God's power and wisdom especially manifest. But why speak of "manifold wisdom"? The Greek word is *polypoikilos,* "much variegated." Eubulus uses it to refer to the various shades of color in a garland of flowers. Euripides employs the word to describe the variety of colors in a robe. Chrysostom observed that the meaning is not "varied" only but "much varied." Says Eadie,[5] "The wisdom described by the remarkable epithet is not merely deep or great wisdom, but wisdom illustrious for its very numerous forms, and for the strange diversity yet perfect harmony of its myriads of aspects and methods of operation."

Who but God in His wisdom would have thought of saving man by becoming man in Christ His Son? The wisdom of God in the virgin birth! So Christ was the sinless Son of God, though man. The wisdom of God shown by the humiliation and death of the Son! The wisdom displayed in the resurrection which de-

[5] *Ibid.*

clared Christ to be God's Son and, at the same time, assured us
that we shall rise from our graves! The simple fundamentals of
the Church of Christ as set forth by baptism, a symbol of our
salvation; and by communion, a sign of our continuation in the
faith, declare divine wisdom. Then the preaching of the Cross of
Christ is God's wisdom in method. Says I Corinthians 1:21b,
"It pleased God by the foolishness of preaching to save them that
believe."

And this "manifold wisdom of God" is made known.

a. To High Principalities (3:10a).

"The Principalities," *tais archais,* are angelic beings who have
first rank as *arche,* beginning, would indicate. "The powers,"
tais exousiais, the authorities, are likewise heavenly beings who
are vested with authority. Probably these two designations stand
for all that order of personalities that are above man and yet not
God. Certainly these creatures often have beheld in wonder the
wisdom of God, but what God has wrought in and through the
church excels all else of His doing.

b. "By the Church" (3:10b).

Samuel J. Stone in 1865 was illuminated to express in sacred
verse something of the wonder and glory of the Church when he
wrote:

> "The Church's one foundation
>   Is Jesus Christ her Lord;
> She is His new creation
>   By water and the word:
> From Heaven He came and sought her,
>   To be His holy bride;
> With His own blood He bought her,
>   And for her life He died.

"Elect from every nation,
    Yet one o'er all the earth,
Her charter of salvation,
    One Lord, one faith, one birth;
One holy name she blesses,
    Partakes one holy food,
And to one hope she presses,
    With every grace endued.

"Mid toil and tribulation,
    And tumult of her war,
She waits the consummation
    Of peace forevermore;
Till, with the vision glorious,
    Her longing eyes are blest,
And the great church victorious
    Shall be the church at rest.

"Yet she on earth hath union
    With God the Three in One,
And mystic sweet communion
    With those whose rest is won:
Oh happy ones and holy!
    Lord, give us grace that we,
Like them, the meek and lowly,
    On high may dwell with Thee."

5. THE MAGNITUDE OF THE MYSTERY (3:11, 12)

a. It is Included in God's Eternal Purpose (3:11).

One's purpose is what he proposes to do. The Greek for "purpose" is *prothesis,* from *pro,* before and *tithemi,* to place. Hence the literal meaning is that which is placed before the mind. Man's purposes are circumscribed by his human limitations, but God's intentions are realized because of His might and foresight.

One of the arguments for the existence of God is the teleological or that which sees a divine purpose, or a directing intelligence, back of all nature. God must have had an end in view as He wrought and thought, and in His purpose was the plan for the church.

And this is eternal, *ton aionon,* of the ages. Eadie judges this expression to be equivalent to *aionios,* well rendered, eternal, or everlasting. Time is required for the maturing and perfecting of judgments and plans. "Snap judgments" are usually short lived. So as we ponder the divine plan of God as wrought out in and by the Church, we will marvel again and again at its glorious perfection. Little wonder that as 5:27 says, Christ will "present it to himself a glorious church."

b. Our Confidence in Christ Makes Us Bold to Embrace This Teaching (3:12).

As verse twelve says of Christ Jesus, "In whom we have boldness and access with confidence by the faith of him." Our confidence (Greek *pepoithesei*) is based on a "persuasion." And when one is persuaded he has been advised. Hence reference is made to the thinking. And note that this attitude of mind that we Christians have is "by the faith of him," or better, through the faith (which we have) in Him. "Of Him" is an objective genitive here. It is our trust in Him based upon His appeal to our heart and mind that enables us to be so confident.

This admiration of Jesus Christ our Lord is held not only by the devoted who accept the fundamental view of Christianity but some who present what E. Y. Mullins terms[6] "opposing theories," vie with one another in lauding the virtues of the Son of God. Renan wrote: "Jesus is in every respect unique, and nothing can be compared with Him. Be the unlooked for phenomena of the

---

[6] E. Y. Mullins. *Why is Christianity True?* (American Baptist Publication Society, Philadelphia, 1905).

future what they may Jesus will not be surpassed. Noble Initiator, repose now in thy glory! Thy work is finished, thy divinity established." Strauss, not an evangelical, said that Christ is "the highest object we can possibly imagine with respect to religion, the Being without whose presence in the mind perfect piety is impossible." Mullins also quotes Prof. G. J. Romanes, J. S. Mill, Goethe, and Matthew Arnold who write in a similar vein, and Sidney Lanier has portrayed Christ thus:

> "But thee, but thee, O sovereign seer of time,
> But thee, O poet's Poet, wisdom's tongue,
> But thee, O man's best Man, O love's best Love,
> O perfect life in perfect labour writ,
> O all men's Comrade, Servant, King, or Priest,—
> What *if* or *yet,* what mole, what flaw, what lapse.
> What least defect or shadow of defect,
> What rumour tattled by an enemy,
> Of inference loose, what lack of grace
> Even in torture's grasp, or sleep or death's—
> O, what amiss may I forgive in thee,
> Jesus, good Paragon, thou Crystal Christ?"

Charles Wesley, the sweet singer of Methodism, in his greatest hymn, "Jesus Lover of my Soul," gives us his estimate in the striking lines:

> Thou, O Christ, art all I want;
> More than all in Thee I find;
>
> * * * * *
>
> Just and holy is thy name,
>
> * * * * *
>
> Thou art full of truth and grace.

Little wonder that Paul can say, "In whom we have boldness and access." The Greek word for "boldness" is *parrhesia,* composed of *pan,* all or every, and *rhesis,* speaking. Hence the root meaning is freedom in speaking or as Eadie says, "free speech." This word is further defined by "access" which follows. *Prosagogen,* the act of bringing to, or the approach, seems to be the literal rendering of this term. In the epistle to the Hebrews we are urged to hold to our "boldness" (3:6; 10:19,35), in Christian testimony and prayer. What marvelous privileges do we enjoy in this "dispensation of the grace of God."

CHAPTER SUMMARY

THE DISPENSATION OF THE GRACE OF GOD
(Eph. 3:1-12)

1. The Mystery of This Dispensation Was Revealed to Paul for Us (vv. 3-5)

2. The Meaning of This Mystery (v. 6).

3. The Minister of This Mystery (vv. 7-9).
   a. This ministry is a gift (v. 7).
   b. The humility of the minister (v. 8a).
   c. This ministry is definite as to its scope and subject (v. 8b).
   d. This ministry is missionary (v. 9a).
   e. This mystery has been hidden hitherto in God (v. 9b).

4. The Manifestation of the Mystery (v. 10)
   a. To high personalities (v. 10a).
   b. By the church (v. 10).

5. The Magnitude of the Mystery (vv. 11, 12)
   a. It is included in God's eternal purpose (v. 11).
   b. Our confidence in Christ makes us bold to embrace this teaching (v. 12).

CHAPTER VII

A PRAYER WITH A TRIPLE PURPOSE
(Ephesians 3:13-21)

How COMPLETE is the inspired Word of God. Not only "all scripture is given by inspiration of God, and is profitable for doctrine, for reproof, for correction, for instruction in righteousness" (II Tim. 3:16), but evidently sufficient Scripture is available to meet our every need. Take the matter of prayer as an example. We have the prayer that Jesus taught His disciples, "Our Father which art in heaven." We also have His great intercessory prayer recorded in John 17. The former provides the church with a form of prayer suitable for concert praying in worship, the latter discloses to us the heart of our Great High Priest, our Great, Good, and Chief Shepherd, in His intercession for us, His followers, His flock. And is it not fitting and significant to us who would be instructed in prayer that the Apostle to the Gentiles has also left us a record of two of his prayers, one in Ephesians 1:15-23 and the other in Ephesians 3:13-21. Each is of the same length and each is following a revelation of the believers special blessings in Christ. We pause here to recall that as Paul had bidden farewell to the Ephesian elders, as Acts 20:36-38 records, "He kneeled down, and prayed with them all." And the effect of this was that "They all wept sore, and fell on Paul's neck, and kissed him, Sorrowing most of all for the words which he spake, that they should see his face no more."

In all this Paul is revealed as a pastor, a priest with love and concern for the flock. And may we not find in these prayers recorded in his letter to the Ephesians the sum and substance of his desire for those whom he has led to Christ and taught?

1. THE OCCASION OF THIS PRAYER (3:13)

"Wherefore I desire"; these words at once reveal the burning soul of the apostle and tell us just why he is so exercised. "Wherefore" translates *dio* which is equivalent to *dio touto,* on account of *this:* "This" that he had said regarding the remarkable plan of God being made known "by the church"; "this" that he had said regarding the Church being bold in testimony and confident in prayer. "This" is why he is exercised. (See 3:8-12.) "I desire," *aitoumai,* is literally I ask. The form is in the middle voice and hence means earnest or intensive asking. An example of this is seen when Herod had offered the daughter of Herodias anything to the half of his kingdom because her dance had pleased him. Whereupon the girl went to her mother saying, "What shall I ask?" *Ti aitesomai?* With enthusiasm she uttered the question (Mark 6:24). When in James 4:2 we read, "Ye have not, because ye ask not" we might think of this as, "Ye have not because there is no earnestness in your asking," *me aiteisthai hymas.* Their prayer is too perfunctory. Hence they do not have the answer. But with Paul there is deep desire and keen concern, occasioned by:

a. THE FAINT-HEARTED EPHESIANS (3:13a).

"I desire that ye faint not." "Faint" translates *enkakein; kakos* means bad; hence our term means to behave badly, that is to come short of one's best behavior as he does when weary. Moulton and Milligan[1] cite an instance where the word means "cowardice." As we study this great prayer we will see that its import is that these Christians might be stabilized by "him that is able to do exceeding abundantly above all that we ask or think, according to the power that worketh in us."

This very morning a friend was recounting to me the trials

[1] Moulton and Milligan. *Vocabulary of Greek N. T.*

of Nebraska farmers due to hail, locusts, etc. Said she, "Those who were religious could stick it out better than those who had no religion." She meant that God kept them courageous. Life's vicissitudes call for a hardihood that only God can give.

b. A Misinterpretation of "Tribulations" (3:13b).

These Ephesians were prone to lose heart at Paul's afflictions. But said he of his afflictions, "which is your glory." Now "glory," translating *doxa,* means the resplendent, the thing seen favorably. By this term Paul sublimates his trials as he does elsewhere in this letter. He is "the prisoner of the Lord," rather than of Nero (4:1). He is "an ambassador in a chain" rather than a tethered prisoner (6:20). He is divinely enabled to glorify the commonplace. So the Christian lifts even death, the last enemy, out of the category of the curse and calls it a "sleep." As the author of Hebrews says, "No chastening for the present seemeth to be joyous, but grievous: nevertheless, afterward it yieldeth the peaceable fruits of righteousness unto them that are exercised thereby" (Heb. 12:11). And we glory in the hardships that our parents and heroes have suffered courageously rather than in their comfort and ease.

2. THE POSTURE OF THE ONE WHO PRAYS (13:14a)

Instead of saying, "I pray for you," Paul says, "I bow my knees," *kampto ta gonata mou.* This expression is used in Romans 11:4 to apply to the seven thousand men who had not worshipped the image of Baal. It describes an attitude of reverence reflected by the posture. In the presence of Christ knelt the father of the lunatick (Matt. 17:14), the leper (Mark 1:40), and the rich young ruler (Mark 10:17). Kant says that this posture signifies servility, and Calvin remarks that one who bows denotes the thing by the sign. And "bowing" is not only befitting to the oriental but is becoming to all of us. In fact, "every knee shall bow and every tongue confess that Jesus Christ is Lord." So Paul's posture bespeaks a heart attitude that God will note with favour.

And observe *"For this cause* I bow," *Toutou charin* is the Greek here. *Charin* usually means grace or favor but in this place is a preposition meaning *favorable to* which we have toned down to because of or on account of. And "this," *toutou,* points to the contents of verse thirteen. In keeping with the thought of Paul's strong desire that there be no fainting at his tribulations, he bows to pray. So prayer is the Christian's outlet when under pressure. As Psalm 91:15 says, "He shall call upon me, and I will answer him: I will be with him in trouble."

3. THE ONE ADDRESSED IN THIS PRAYER (3:14b, 15)

The apostle does not cringe in the presence of a despot but comes boldly to a throne of grace. He prays to "the Father of our Lord Jesus Christ." As we think of the awesome dread of even Israel, God's chosen people, in the presence of Jehovah, we are grateful that Jesus showed us that God is a Father. Said Jesus, "He that hath seen me hath seen the Father." What reassurance comes with these words as we remember how kind, helpful, and good was Jesus. He was "the Lamb of God" as well as "the Lion of the tribe of Judah."

As the author of Hebrews says, "For ye are not come unto the mount . . . that burned with fire, nor unto blackness, and darkness, and tempest . . . (And so terrible was the sight, that Moses said, I exceedingly fear and quake:) But ye are come unto mount Sion, and unto the city of the living God, the heavenly Jerusalem . . . and to Jesus the mediator of the new covenant, and to the blood of sprinkling, that speaketh better things than that of Abel" (Heb. 12:18-24).

Yes we come to God as our heavenly Father who has spoken to us "by his Son" (Heb. 1:2) or "in Sonship," as the Greek *en whio* literally means. We understand the Father because we have seen and heard the Son. "Philip saith unto him, Lord, shew us the Father, and it sufficeth us. Jesus saith unto him, Have I been so long time with you, and yet hast thou not known me, Philip? he that hath seen me hath seen the Father" (John 14:8,9). And because Jesus is "the express image of God's person" therefore

> "With confidence I now draw nigh
> And Father Abba, Father cry."

To further impress his readers with the accessibility of God, the gracious Father, the Holy Spirit inspires Paul to add "Of whom the whole family in heaven and earth is named." But this verse will require some study. "The whole family" translates *pasa patria*. "Father" in Greek is *pater*. Note the similarity of *patria* and *pater*. Moulton and Milligan[2] say that *patria* is often used in the Septuagint for a group of persons united by descent from a common father, *pater*. Thayer says that each son of Jacob was the head of a *patria* or family. After quoting numerous leading authorities, Eadie says, "The meaning seems to be that every circle of holy and intelligent creatures having the name of *patria*, (family) takes that name from God as *Pater*."

Evidently this precious passage should remind us of the approachable head of a household, family, or clan, who will hear the cases and listen to the petitions of the children as they come with their several needs. Thus Isaac received and heard the

---

[2] *Ibid.*

requests of Esau and Jacob. As a patriarchal father Jacob blessed
the sons of Joseph. And Moses wearied with hearing the causes
of Israel in the wilderness. Bathsheba presented the request for
Solomon to David, the father and king. Every true father pities
and provides for his children. And the family is a divine institution. The very helplessness of the human infant and the
indigence and inexperience of the offspring make the role of
father necessary. God in constituting the universe gave a large
place to fatherhood. And we know of God as we sublimate
"father." "God so loved the world, that he gave his only begotten Son." As Paul argues elsewhere, If God "spared not his
own Son, but delivered him up for us all, how shall he not with
him also freely give us all things?" (Rom. 8:32). Such a conception of God makes for the prayer of faith from the lips of
His children.

4. THE PURPOSES OF THIS PRAYER (3:16-21)

The ultimate purpose of this prayer is clearly set forth in verse
nineteen; namely, "that ye might be filled with all the fulness
of God." But this divine fulness is realized through a clearly
expressed process which we do well to observe. Briefly stated
the purpose of God for each believer includes Christ's indwelling
the child of God, the believer's apprehension of His love, and
hence the fulness of God in the heart.

a. That Christ May Indwell the Believer (3:16, 17a).

The threefold purpose in Paul's prayer may be clearly seen by
a close study of the Greek text. As I see it, "that," at the beginning of verse sixteen, in the middle of verse seventeen, and in
the middle of verse nineteen, marks three different purpose
clauses. Each of these "thats" translates, *hina,* in order that.

Hence my rendering of the main statement of verses fourteen through nineteen is as follows: "I bow my knees . . . in order that (God) may give to you . . . to be strengthened through His Spirit, that is Christ indwelling through faith, in order that you, rooted and grounded in love, may be able to comprehend . . . and to know the love of Christ . . . in order that ye may be filled unto all the fulness of God." This means that Paul prayed that God would grant Christ to indwell the believers through the Holy Spirit that they might comprehend Christ's love so that they may be filled with God's fulness.

Such a rich Christian experience as that described by the words, "That Christ may dwell in your hearts," must come as a gift from our heavenly Father. Ignatius, the venerable bishop of Antioch, when on trial before the emperor was asked what his surname *Theophorus* signified. His reply was, "One who has Christ in his heart." The word "dwell" in verse seventeen translates *katoikesai* which means to settle down or inhabit rather than to sojourn or visit. Eadie explains that this inhabitation is not a mere reception of Christian doctrine nor is it a mystical exaggeration. In Colossians 1:25-27 Paul, in presenting the great doctrine of the "mystery," refers to the "saints: To whom God would make known what is the riches of the glory of this mystery among the Gentiles; which is Christ in you, the hope of glory." The glorious riches of the church is the indwelling Christ whose presence assures us of the reality of the glorious hope of better things to be at the coming of our Lord. So God's love for the world impelled Him not only to give His Son that He might die for us but also that the Son of God might indwell us.

As in the prayer recorded in chapter one, God's power is prominent here. There the petition is that we might "know" the exceeding greatness of His power; here it is that we might be "strengthened with might by his Spirit in the inner man."

"Strengthened," *krataiothenai*, is to have power which one applies. When a Roman prefect visited Oxyrhynchus there was a popular demonstration during which they cried out *eis eona to kratos ton Romaion,* "the Roman power forever!" Here the word signifies dominion. And Thayer in his study of *kratos* as a synonym refers to it as "relative and manifested power." And as used in this connection it is related to "might," *dynamis,* general and inherent power. But this "might" is none other than that which comes "by his Spirit," *dia tou pneumatos.* Now since the Holy Spirit is one member of the Godhead, His power is limitless.

Such power is transferred to the heart of the appropriating Christian. It reaches "the inner man," *eis ton eso anthropon,* which I Peter 3:4 styles, "The hidden man of the heart." This inner hidden strength of the stalwart saint cannot be explained by physical force, nerve energy, or mental acumen. Its miraculous display can be accounted for only by Paul's word to the Philippians, "I can do all things through Christ which strengtheneth me." And observe that this supernatural strength, ministered by deity inhabiting the inner being of man, is realized by appropriating faith, *dia tes pisteos.* True it is "by His Spirit"; but no less true is it that it is "by faith." Fellow Christians, let us believe! Early Christians who stressed faith were called "Pistics" as over against the "Gnostics" who emphasized knowledge. May our trust in God's power for holy living and effective ministry be so prominent as to cause us to honestly wear the title of "Pistics" in this day of materialism, mechanics, and mental emphasis.

b. That the Believer May Comprehend the Love of Christ (3:17b, 18, 19a).

This is the second step in the purpose of this great prayer. According to the arrangement of the words of verse seventeen, it seems evident that to have Christ indwell one by faith is to be "rooted and grounded in love." Thus "love" is the soil in which the Christian is planted. "Rooted," *errizomenoi,* is a perfect participle and as such signifies that we were once rooted and that we stay planted in the soil of divine grace which Christ brings. Now roots convey nourishment to the plant according to the composition of the soil. And being rooted in love the Christian should bear the precious fruit of love. His personality should become increasingly lovely. His deeds should be impelled by love. His thoughts should be charitable. Rapid growth results when the nature of the plant and the character of the soil suit as is the case of the soul born from above abiding in the love of God.

"Rooted" also signifies stability. It is the tap root of the giant oak that enables it to stand erect against the stormy winds. And here Paul introduces another term to reinforce this idea. It is "grounded," *tethemeliomenoi,* which literally means established or founded. It means to have a foundation. Under this figure love is the bed rock upon which the Christian builds. And, in line with consistency, the superstructure of Christian experience and character answers to the substructure of love. And we hasten to say that love here is *agape,* unselfish, altruistic interest in the welfare of others. So to have Christ inhabit the heart is to live the lofty life of love.

And Paul's prayer is to the end that the Ephesians and all Christians "may be able to comprehend . . . and to know the love of Christ, which passeth knowledge." How can we know that "which passeth knowledge?" "Knowledge," of verse nineteen is *gnosis,* which means knowledge gained through experience. And the love of Christ is said to "pass knowledge" which comes through normal life experiences. But "passeth" translates *hyperballousan,* to throw over or pass over, hence to "overpass" or surpass. Human experience is not high enough to come up to the experiences that go with the love of Christ. But being in an atmosphere of love by Christ's indwelling presence we "may be able to comprehend . . . the love of Christ." "Be able" translates *exischuo*. *Ischys* means strength as an endowment. A large elephant or, still better, a diesel engine pictures such power. This idea is further increased in our word by *ex*. Hence it means, as Thayer says, "to be eminently able" or "to have full strength." Said Paul to the Corinthians, "Be ye also enlarged." Love expands. Christian experience awakens dormant powers. The dullard or drone has an awakened interest. Late Justice Oliver Wendell Holmes was trailing along as number thirty in his class at Harvard, but suddenly he was seen to advance with a burst of speed and graduated as a Phi Beta Kappa. When President Roosevelt visited him in his ninety-second year, he addressed him as, "The leading American citizen." Justice Holmes was reading Plato as he said, "to improve my mind." So Paul prays for unusual power for the Ephesians "to comprehend," *katala-besthai*. This verb in first century Greek meant to "appropriate." And so Paul uses it, say Moulton and Milligan. And to appropriate is to make something one's own.

Now to encompass all the love of Christ is quite an order. And lest there would be some possibility of limiting this love, Paul specifies "the breadth, and length, and depth, and height" of Christ's love. These four dimensions of divine love have provoked "many wits to run riot in their geometrical and moral discourse upon these dimensions" as Eadie observes by quoting. He agrees with Cramer, Bengel, Steer, and others in the "Assembly's Annotations," who suppose that the allusion is to the Christian temple. It is evident that this figure is present in other parts of the prayer. He prays that Christ may "dwell" in our hearts, and that we have love as a foundation. At the end of the previous chapter a "holy temple" is in view. And since this temple is composed of regenerated men and women, it seems reasonable to conclude that we see the "breadth" of Christ's love, as we note His love for "all the world"; its "length," as we behold how He loves from age to age; its "depth," as we read of His descent from the highest heaven to the deepest depths of human woe and sin; and its "height," as we contemplate the glory that awaits those who will go to be with Him in the place which He has prepared for them. When such love is comprehended by entering with Christ into His plan and program of taking the gospel to the nations and serving mankind wherever we are, then shall we know, *ginosko,* by personal experience the love of Christ. As said Paul, "The love of Christ constraineth us."

c. That the Believer May "be Filled with all the Fulness of God" (3:19b).

This is the ultimate purpose of Paul's prayer—God's fulness in the believer. But how can any church contain all there is of divine fulness? We are helped in solving this problem by remembering that in 1:23 we read of the church as being Christ's body, "the fulness of him that filleth all in all." It seems easier to think of Christ's being the Head of the church than to conceive of the church as His body. But such it is. In I Corinthians 12:12 we read, "For as the body is one, and hath many members, and all the members of that one body, being many, are one body: so also is Christ." In this passage, "Christ" means the mystical Christ of which the Lord Jesus is the Head and we members.

That God does count upon the church to contain His virtues and manifest His graces, we infer from the statement of Ephesians 3:10 which declares that the manifold wisdom of God might be made known by the church. We are helped to understand just how any church may have divine fulness by recalling Paul's word to the Corinthians, "I thank my God always on your behalf, for the grace of God which is given you by Jesus

Christ; That in everything ye are enriched by him, in all utterance, and in all knowledge; *So that ye come behind in no gift"* (I Cor. 1:4,5,7). If a church comes behind in no gift of the Spirit of God, that company of Christians embodies all that God has in mind for His people. And so to these same Corinthians Paul specifies as to particular gifts when he says: "Now ye are the body of Christ, and members in particular. And God hath set some in the church, first apostles, secondarily prophets, thirdly teachers, after that miracles, then gifts of healings, helps, governments, diversities of tongues" (I Cor. 12:27, 28).

When we think of Christ what does He mean to us? Is it not just this, the manifestation of God, the Father? And, of Christ, John writes, "Of his fulness have all we received, and grace for grace." And why have we of the church been chosen? Listen to Peter, the mouth-piece of the apostolic group as he declares, "But ye are a chosen generation, a royal priesthood, a holy nation, a peculiar people; that ye should show forth the praises, (*aretas*, virtues or excellencies) of him who hath called you out of darkness unto his marvelous light" (I Peter 2:9).

So we conclude that Paul's purpose in praying for this church is that it may have all gifts and graces that are requisite to manifesting God to the world. It is related that one of the Gordons, known for his saintliness, one day called upon a lad who was ill. When the mother, who had been absent, returned her little son said to her, "Mother, Jesus was here." She replied that the visitor could not have been Jesus. But the boy, whose heart had been satisfied, insisted that his guest answered to the description of the Son of God. If Gordon were not the Christ, he was a godly Christian. When each member of the church has had Christ thus formed in him, then it can be truly said of that company of believers that it is "filled with all the fulness of God."

5. PROPER PRAISE AFTER SUCH PETITIONS
(3:20,21)

a. GOD's OMNIPOTENCE RECOGNIZED (3:20).

After contemplating that the Lord's chief aim for us is that we might be filled with His fulness, we join with Paul in the doxology of verses 20 and 21—And to Him who is powerful enough to do beyond all things which we earnestly ask or think according to the power which energizes us, to Him be the glory by the church and by Christ Jesus unto all the generations of the age of the ages; Amen.

Our asking may be ever so eager as the middle voice *aitoumetha,* suggests. And our thinking may exceed our requests since thoughts surpass words, yet God's power surpasses both our poor prayers and our highest and holiest aspirations. And we rejoice that this divine dynamic energizes and motivates us for good. Here is that unaccounted for reserve of power, that full reservoir of force of which Jesus spake on "the last day, that great day of the feast," when He *"cried* saying, If any man thirst, let him come unto me, and drink. He that believeth on me, as the Scripture hath said, out of his belly shall flow rivers of living water. (But this spake he of the Spirit, which they that believe on him should receive . . .)" (John 7:37-39).

b. GOD's GLORY IN TIME AND IN ETERNITY (3:21).

To the first question of the Shorter Catechism, "What is man's chief end?" the answer is, "Man's chief end is to glorify God and enjoy Him forever." But alas, man has not glorified God as he should. In His great intercessory prayer of John seventeen, Jesus says, "I have glorified thee on the earth. I have finished the work which thou gavest me to do." How better can we glorify God than by doing His will and work? Jesus did always those things that pleased the Father. In Gethsemane as He faced the Cross, He reverently prayed, "Thy will be done."

But our doxology states that God will be glorified "by the church" as well as by Christ. The bride shares with the heavenly Groom in lauding the Lord, in doing His will, in serving Him.

CHAPTER SUMMARY

A PRAYER WITH A TRIPLE PURPOSE
(Eph. 3:13-21)

1. The Occasion of This Prayer (v. 13)
   a. The faint-hearted Ephesians (v. 13a).
   b. A misinterpretation of "tribulations" (v. 13b).

2. The Posture of the One Who Prays (v. 14a).

3. The One Addressed in This Prayer (vv. 14b, 15).

4. The Purposes of This Prayer (vv. 16-21)
   a. That Christ may indwell the believers (vv. 16, 17a).
   b. That the believer may comprehend the love of Christ (vv. 17b-19a).
   c. That the believer may "be filled with all the fulness of God" (v. 19).

5. Proper Praise After Such Petitions (vv. 20, 21)
   a. God's omnipotence recognized (v. 20).
   b. God's glory in time and in eternity (v. 21).

Chapter VIII

WALKING WORTHILY TO PROMOTE UNITY
(Ephesians 4:1-16)

THIS PARTICULAR subject might be used to cover the contents of Ephesians throughout chapters four, five, and six. However, under it we will develop only 4:1-16.

1. THE CHARACTERISTICS OF SUCH A WALK (4:1,2)

To conduct ourselves in a manner becoming to our high calling is the primary exhortation of Paul, the prince of apostles. That he believes we should live on a high plane during our earthly pilgrimage may be inferred from the manner in which he sublimates his own life experiences. Though he writes from a Roman prison, yet he styles himself the prisoner "in the Lord" (4:1, R.V.).

His bondage is permitted by Christ and is due to his having preached the gospel of Christ. He spends no time chafing under the Roman yoke, nor does the chain which manacles his hand hinder the writing of this epistle. He soars though in a cage.

What a challenge to us. Our conduct should be in keeping with our calling; and, as such, it should manifest the humbler virtues. Hence we are called to manifest "lowliness . . . meekness . . . long-suffering" by "forbearing one another in love" in order "to keep the unity of the Spirit in the bond of peace" (4:2,3).

Thus our aim as Christians should be peaceful unity. So desirous of this should we be as to be "endeavoring to keep" it.

At once we observe the large place given to Christian forbearance. Humility, meekness, and patience are requisites to forbearance without which there can be no unity. Efforts towards church union are many and with good intentions. The Master prayed that His disciples might be "one . . . that the world may believe" (John 17:21). The prominence here given to forbearance through humility, meekness, and patience instructs us as to how unity may be maintained. It is a thing of life and spirit rather than something of external uniformity. In 4:16 the figure of the human body is introduced to make plain the vital relation of the different members of the Body of Christ, the Church, one to another. In brief that verse says, "The whole body . . . maketh increase of the body." Each part contributes to each other part and so to the whole. Some lowly hidden work some members of the body must perform. And in case of a well coordinated physical body achieving some success we give credit to the body as a whole. If an athlete wins a race we name him as the winner. We seldom stop to recount what part was performed by his eyes, his heart, his lungs, his leg muscles, etc. So in the Body of Christ, each member should cooperate even as an unobserved "joint," that the race may be not slowed down.

2. THE OBJECT OF SUCH A WALK—UNITY
(4:3-16)

a. IDEAL UNITY (4:4-6).

Paul enumerates the sevenfold oneness of believers when he says, "There is one body, and one Spirit . . . one hope of your calling; One Lord, one faith, one baptism, One God and Father of all, who is above all, and through all, and in you all" (4:4-6). "One body," of which each Christian is a member, (I Cor. 12:12); "one Spirit," by which we are all baptized into that one body (I Cor. 12:13); "one hope," that "When he shall appear, we shall be like him," (I John 3:2,3); "one Lord," to whom every knee shall bow and every tongue shall confess, (Phil. 2:10,11); "one faith," whose content is the gospel of Jesus Christ, (Rom. 1:16; I Cor. 15:3,4); "one baptism," which is the Lord's way through the Spirit, of bringing each one into the Body of Christ, (I Cor. 12:13); "one God and Father," who is "God of all" in that He is the only true God, who is "Father of all" who have received the Spirit of adoption, whereby we cry, "Abba, Father," (Rom. 8:15) and all of us who have accepted Christ as our Saviour and Lord, bear the same relation to God. He is "above all." All must recognize His lordship. He is "through all." No one alone expresses God to the world but each participates in making Him known to the world, just as each member of the human body unites in manifesting the wishes of the will. He is "in you all" and hence no one has a monopoly on the Spirit of God.

We hasten to observe that there is point in recounting this actual unity. To recognize the unity inherent in the Christian system is to be persuaded that we who are sharers in it do well to cooperate in maintaining it. For since each of us has a will and is capable of individual decision and action it is necessary that each one consciously give himself to the realization of the divine oneness if God's purposes are to be accomplished. We are not parts of a machine nor are we automata.

b. Unity in Diversity (4:7-11).

"But unto every one of us is given grace according to the measure of the gift of Christ." Thus Paul introduces his discussion on diversities of gifts. "But," *de,* could be rendered "and." The term is both conjunctive and adversative in its meaning. The "unity" under consideration in 4:4-6 is carried into these verses but there is a new element introduced. This is not disunity but dissimilarity in unity. Not every one receives "grace" in equal measure. The "measure of the gift of Christ" determines the grace required and bestowed.

And since "He . . . gave gifts unto men," and not just one gift, we have variety as expressed by verse eleven, which declares, "He gave . . . apostles, prophets . . . evangelists, and some, pastors and teachers (pastor-teachers)." These are not all of Christ's gifts but these are the ones intended for the purpose of bringing about that unity of which we are thinking.

Paul interrupts the progress of thought to give us the Christological passages of verses 9 and 10. In effect these verses stress the importance of Christ's incarnation being prior to His ascension and the necessity of the descended Son of God being the very same Person as the ascended Saviour of men. As Hebrews 2:9 says, "We see Jesus, who was made a little lower than the angels for the suffering of death, crowned with glory and honour." The Jesus "Who was made . . . lower," was crowned upon His ascension and as a victorious Monarch He gave gifts for the benefit of men.

Do we recognize these "gifted" men specified in verse eleven, as having come from the ascended Christ? Do we receive the messages of all of them? Or are we partial to evangelists and prejudiced against teachers? Some church people profess to accept Paul, the apostle, but care little for a Moody, or a Chapman, or a Billy Sunday. Yet He gave not one kind of gift but several "gifts." We recall that chapter four opens with an exhortation. Paul beseeches us to "walk" or conduct ourselves in a manner befitting our calling. Then he specifies that we should embody loving forbearance, realized by humility, meekness and longsuffering, in our eagerness to guard the unity of the Spirit.

A Christian layman once said that in every home there should be two *bears,* bear and forbear. In the interest of peace we must learn to bear or "put up with" one another.

"And he gave some apostles; some prophets," as the Authorized Version has in 4:11, might lead some to think that the ascended Christ gave apostles to some, prophets to some and evangelists to others. But the Greek text literally rendered has it "And he himself gave both the apostles and the prophets," or "And he himself gave some as apostles and some as prophets." Christ gave all the various gifts to all as the succeeding verses make clear.

c. Unity Realized (4:12-16).

Christ's life and work are purposeful. "The Son of man is come to seek and to save that which was lost" (Luke 19:10), expresses the great aim of His incarnation. He gave gifts for a purpose. Let us observe,

(1) The ultimate aim (v. 13). This is to bring us all "in the unity of the faith, and of the (full) knowledge (Gr. *epignosis*) of the Son of God, unto a fullgrown (Gr. *teleios*) man, unto the measure of the stature of the fulness of Christ" (4:13 R.V.).

What a challenge to us Christians is this. Nothing short of "the measure of the stature of the fulness of Christ" will suffice for us if we would be as He desires. And this will be our size spiritually if we be mature. And the mature church will be comprised of members who have attained "the unity of the faith and of the knowledge of the Son of God." This means that we are united in our faith in the Son of God and that we all have full knowledge of the Son of God. We trust Christ whom we know.

That the aim here has to do primarily with each member of the church being fortified in knowledge, may be seen by noting verse fourteen. Paul employs the figure of contrast and sets forth the dangers that lurk for "children" in faith and knowledge. These are "tossed to and fro" as waves of the sea. A new "wind of doctrine" agitates them. Deceivers victimize them by their cunning arts, and they find themselves in a brainstorm of doubt and indecision. How important to be established in the great doctrines of the church such as the virgin birth of Christ, the deity of our Lord, and the resurrection of the body. Failure to be in agreement on the fundamentals of the faith of the Church of Christ is sure to lead to divisions which Jesus deplored and against which He prayed in that prayer of prayers for His disciples in which an outstanding petition was, "That they all may be one; as thou, Father, art in me, and I in thee, that they also may be one in us: that the world may believe that thou hast sent me" (John 17:21). The figures used in verse fourteen are very suggestive. "Tossed to and fro" portrays the light, frothy foam of the surface rather than the quiet waters of the deep. "Slight of men and cunning craftiness" picture the evil devices of false teachers which succeed in ensnaring gullible and immature babes in Christ.

(2) *The necessary process* (*v. 16*). In order to realize the aim of unity of faith and knowledge, Paul evidently has in mind a process. He sets this forth in the figure of the growth, development, and maturity of the human body. He sees an analogy between this physical and mundane process and "the edifying of the body of Christ" (4:12). In 1:22,23 we are told that the church is Christ's body. Verse sixteen describes the unity of the human body and the cooperation of its several members. The parts of the body are constructed so that they can be "fitly joined together." The Unseen Architect has planned the relative sizes and shapes of all in keeping with their places and functions in the body as a whole, but the bones of a mere skeleton fall apart. Hence the need of their being "compacted" by "that which every joint supplieth."

And as in the case of the human body so it is with the Body of Christ, the Church. Each member should supply that which will make for a spiritual organism. As the main statement of verse sixteen puts it, "The whole body . . . maketh increase of the body unto the edifying of itself in love." The heart pumps the blood throughout the whole body after it has been purified in the lungs with air taken in through the nostrils. And if the lips, teeth, tongue, esophagus, stomach, intestines, and other organs had not contributed their services in mastication, digestion, and assimilation of food there would be no blood for the heart to pump. Truly the body builds up the body. And just as certainly we need various members in the body of Christ to edify the Church. The minister of the Word of God feeds us with the "sincere milk of the Word," the "Bread of Life," the "strong meat," and the humblest "member" should make his contribution. As Jude 20,21 exhorts, "But ye, beloved, building up yourselves on your most holy faith, praying in the Holy Ghost, Keep yourselves in the love of God." Writing on this very subject at greater length in I Corinthians 12, Paul says in verse 28, "And God hath set some in the church, first apostles, secondarily prophets, thirdly teachers, after that miracles, then gifts of healings, helps, governments, diversities of tongues." So it is a case of "having gifts differing." But whatever be the gift it should be used for the profit of all.

To disregard this God-given plan for the building up and unifying of His Church is to utterly fail. Sam Jones pictured the preacher as a horse between the shafts of a one horse chaise while the congregation was sitting on top and applying the lash. Pretty heavy hauling I would say. But when we all pull together no load is too large. We can all be "helps" at least.

(3) Prepared implements (v. 12). Rather recently the word "implement" has come into its own as a verb. We speak of God implementing Himself with His servants, as though they were His tools. And we are willing to be even "broken and empty vessels for the Master's use." In this connection we must study

verses 11 and 12 together: "He gave some, apostles; and some, prophets; and some, evangelists; and some, pastors and teachers; For the perfecting of the saints, for the work of the ministry, for the edifying of the body of Christ." "Perfecting" is a translation of the Greek *katartismon,* found first in the New Testament in Matthew 4:21 where it is rendered "mending." Zebedee, James, and John were repairing their nets so those implements, so necessary to a fisherman, would serve their purpose. This word is used in Galatians 6:1 where we are admonished to "restore" a brother overtaken in a fault. Just as a net must be made to be as it ought to be to do what it was intended to do so the fallen brother must be brought back to a cleansed and victorious state in order to function as God intended. This is clearly expressed in Hebrews 13:20,21 in the great prayer of benediction: "And now the God of peace . . . make you perfect in every good work to do his will, working in you that which is well-pleasing in his sight through Jesus Christ." In order to do God's will these Hebrew Christians must be "mended," "restored" to their former Christian experience. So "perfecting" in Ephesians 4:12 signifies the preparing of the saints so that they can function efficiently in doing the work of ministering necessary to the edification of the church.

When I was a lad my mother was a member of a Presbyterian church which conducted "preparatory services" before "Communion Sabbath." This program may have implied a spiritual lack or disrepair on the part of the membership. The strategy of the revivalist has ever been to preach to the membership of the church for a week or more before addressing the unsaved so as to get the converted into such a state of grace that they would be wings rather than weights in his meetings. But "perfecting" does not necessarily imply a restoration from guilt to forgiveness. Wynne would translate Matthew 4:21 and Mark 1:19, "folding their nets," and Wycliffe has it, "making nets."

This recalls to us the use of our Greek root in II Timothy 3:16,17 where we read of the uses of "all scripture" as well as its inspiration. Paul states that Scripture contains doctrine, ministers reproof, offers correction, and provides instruction in righteousness in order that the man of God may be "perfect" (Gr. *artios*) or apt for his work. The following expression, "throughly furnished unto every good work," carries out the idea of aptitude and readiness for service.

What Paul gives as the results of applying the "Scripture" to our lives in II Timothy 3:16,17 is similar to what he gives as the purpose of God's giving to us apostles, prophets, evangelists, pastors, and teachers in Ephesians 4:11,12. The Word of God properly utilized prepares us for every good work; the messages and ministrations of God's gifts, apostles, prophets, etc., prepare us for the work of ministering as may be connected with the upbuilding of the church. We should read the Bible for spiritual food and for counsel for our personal problems as well as for its educational value. For it is recognized that no one ignorant of the Bible is truly educated regardless of the number of degrees that may be after his name. We must give ear to prophets and teachers in order to be able to do the Lord's work intelligently. Tom Paine wrote the first part of *The Age of Reason,* in which he criticized the Bible without having read the New Testament. Had he a right to criticize what he did not know? Other adverse critics of the Scriptures would reverse their positions if they could broaden and deepen their knowledge. But to return to our consideration of what preachers do for us, I recall learning that a Christian layman, who has given millions to the carrying on of the work of training young men and women for Christian service, was brought into this important ministry by the Bible teaching of one of God's gifted teachers.

Kimball told D. L. Moody, then a young Christian, that the world has yet to see what God would do through a man wholly yielded to Him. By God's grace Moody became that man, and through Mr. Moody, C. T. Studd, the great English cricket player, among a million others, was won to Christ. One day Studd was to address the students of Cornell University. John R. Mott, an athlete, who seldom went to chapel, decided to hear the English cricket player. As he entered the auditorium Studd announced as his text, "Seekest thou great things for thyself? Seek them not" (Jer. 45:5). This pierced the heart of Mott with an arrow of conviction. He promised God to engage in Y.M.C.A. work for a year. As the world knows he became a missionary statesman. He was "perfected" by God's prophet.

Ephesians 4:11,12 is in line with such an association as that represented by Elisha and "the sons of the prophets" (II Kings 6:1) or that of Jesus and His twelve disciples (Mark 3:14). Elisha, a disciple of Elijah, was a leader among the prophets. As they sought his counsel as to the place and size of their dwelling we may infer that his words were as the revelation of God to them. And Jesus desired His disciples to be "with Him" not merely for fellowship and comfort but also for instruction. First, they were "ordained" to be with him and second, to be sent forth. There was "The training of the Twelve," as A. B. Bruce expresses it, and then the commission, "Go ye into all the world, and preach the gospel to every creature" (Mark 16:15). In all this we sense a reason for "Bible Schools" or "Bible Institutes." In the names of a number of these schools the word training is prominent. Training aids in doing. "Practical Christian Work" is an important requirement in the curricula of these schools of the Bible. The students learn by practice as well as precept.

Now this program of training implies guidance or instruction and direction. And just at this point the teacher is indispensable in the interest of greatest efficiency. It is recognized that there is informal as well as formal education. The former is sometimes uneconomical and unsystematic, while formal education with its well chosen curriculum, trained teachers, and up-to-date equipment is apparently more efficient in preparing the pupil for life's work by providing him with sample life problems and aiding him in their solution.

Prof. Seeley, in *Ecce Homo*,[1] shows that the teacher is a help to the pupil as an example and an encouragement. The scholar sees in his pedagogue the embodiment of what he would become and is encouraged to pursue his course of study in order to achieve the same success as his instructor. He thinks that he can accomplish his objective since another has done so.

All this which smacks of pedagogy I see latent in God's plan for "the perfecting of the saints." Certainly the apostles, pioneers of the faith; the prophets who, like their Master, speak with authority; the evangelists, who persuade us that the gospel is good news; and the pastor-teachers, who sense our particular need and supply that; all these minister to our upbuilding and training for service.

Without this ministry by these gifts of God, how poorly equipped would we be. Peter denied his Lord, but Jesus looked at him, and he went out and wept bitterly in penitence. See him at Pentecost the essence of fidelity and courage preaching that Christ whom He had failed in his timidity. John Wesley, who came to America to convert the Indians, found he had bad need of being converted himself. When he had been impressed by a Moravian and his heart "strangely warmed" what a power for righteousness he became.

Recall that there is "the work of the ministry." "There's a work for you; something for each of us now to do." A church is not called into being by the fiat of Omnipotence but is built by work. The building of the temple of the Lord was a desire first

---

[1] Prof. John Robert Seeley. *Ecce Homo*. (Little, Brown and Company, Boston, 1898).

in David's heart and was later carried to reality by Solomon. But mark the amount of labor necessary to the temple's completion. Ten thousand Israelites were sent to Lebanon each month to work in cedar and fir. "And Solomon had threescore and ten thousand that bare burdens, and fourscore thousand hewers in the mountains . . . (and) three thousand and three hundred, which ruled over the people that wrought in the work" (I Kings 5:15, 16). And there was skilled work that could be done only by the Sidonians who also wrought. But what a temple was constructed! Says Paul in I Corinthians 3:9, "For we are labourers together with God: . . . ye are God's building." And Peter employs the same figure when he says, "Ye also, as lively stones, are built up a spiritual house" (I Pet. 2:5). Who would not wish to spend and be spent to erect a spiritual temple of God?

(4) THE TECHNIQUE (4:15)

It is to be observed that we are told what to do and how to do it in order to come "unto a perfect man, unto the measure of the stature of the fulness of Christ." Verse 15 states, "But speaking the truth in love, may grow up into him in all things, which is the head, even Christ." Here we have our technique, the method by which we accomplish our desired end. It is truth that must be spoken. Said Jesus to Pilate, "To this end was I born, and for this cause came I into the world, that I should bear witness unto the truth" (John 18:37). Said He to Thomas, "I am the way, the truth, and the life" (John 14:6). So the Christian spokesman must be an apostle and a prophet of truth. But truth may be spoken harshly in bitterness. Oh, the word battles of those who "contend for the faith" to the point of hating their hearers. We are to speak the truth "in love."

Christ was "the Word" of God's love. He declared by word, deed, and life, the truth of God. He was the divine embodiment of the love of God. "For God so loved the world, that he gave his only begotten Son, that whosoever believeth in him should not perish, but have everlasting life" (John 3:16).

Paul's classic on love in I Corinthians 13 with its great climax, "And now abideth faith, hope, love, these three; but the greatest of these is love;" his exhortation to "Let love be without hypocrisy" (Romans 12:9 R.V.); his statement, "The fruit of the Spirit is love" (Gal. 5:22); these all express the apostle's high estimate of love. And John, who is content in his gospel account to style himself, "One of his disciples, whom Jesus loved" (John 13:23; 19:26), lays emphasis upon love. He reports that Jesus' weeping as He approached Lazarus' grave was interpreted by the Jews with the words, "Behold how he loved him!" (John 11:36). Before narrating the incident of Jesus' washing the disciples' feet John remarks, "Having loved his own which were in the world, he loved them unto the end (Dr. *eis telos,* unto the uttermost)" (John 13:1). But in his old age as he writes his first epistle he sums up the burden of his heart by saying, "Beloved, if God so loved us, we ought also to love one another" (I John 4:11). In the eighteen verses which comprise the immediate context of this passage we find love used twenty-nine times. And the kind of love urged upon us is not a sentimental fondness one for the other but rather a thoughtful altruistic attitude which leads to deeds of kindness and helpfulness. This the Greek word *agape* signifies. In his booklet, "His Love,"[2] Dr. Norman B. Harrison relates that as Dr. J. H. Jowett was crossing the Atlantic he found himself at the spot where the Titanic went down. When told how far below the surface it was; too deep down for man to recover, Dr. Jowett reflected: "Then I thought of all the human wreckage engulfed and sunk in oceanic depths of sin. Very far down. But not too far down for the Love of God! He descended into hell; and He will descend again if you are there.

[2] Norman B. Harrison. *His Love.* (Harrison Service, Minneapolis).

'If I make my bed in hell—Thou art there'; 'He bore our sin'; then He got beneath it. And there is no human wreckage lying in the ooze of the deepest sea of iniquity that His deep love cannot reach and redeem."

And God's apostles, prophets, evangelists, and pastor-teachers spend and are spent to add to and edify the body of Christ, the Church. Paul held not his life dear unto himself. He was "in jeopardy every hour." Said he, "I die daily." He was of them who

> "Pour out their lives like the rush of a river,
> Wasting its waters forever and ever."

Jeremiah was imprisoned in the mire from which he could be extricated only by man power other than his own. White-field's life burned out as the candle which he held burned low in his hand while he preached once again after an all too strenuous day. "Speaking the truth in love" is the divine method of building up the body of Christ.

CHAPTER SUMMARY

WALKING WORTHILY TO PROMOTE UNITY
(Eph. 4:1-16)

1. The Characteristics of Such a Walk (vv. 1, 2)
2. The Object of Such a Walk—Unity (vv. 3-16)
   a. Ideal unity as a basis (vv. 4-6).
   b. Unity in diversity (vv. 7-11).
   c. Unity realized (vv. 12-16).
      (1) The ultimate aim (v. 13).
      (2) The necessary process—edifying (vv. 12, 16).
      (3) The prepared implements.
      (4) The technique employed (vv. 15, 16)—"speaking the truth in love"
      Thus "the whole body . . . maketh increase of the body," as does the human organism as a unit.

CHAPTER IX

THE HEAVENLY WALK
(Ephesians 4:17-24)

THE CHRISTIAN life is in contrast to the worldly life. Paul probably does not command the Ephesians not to "walk as other Gentiles walk" but affirms and testifies that they do not do so. By definition the church means "the called out" ones (Gr. *ecclesia*). "If any man be in Christ, he is a new creature" (II Cor. 5:17). "Be ye not unequally yoked together with unbelievers . . . Wherefore come out from among them, and be ye separate, saith the Lord" (II Cor. 6:14, 17).

We shall see that those who are walking worthily, or living as befits their Christian calling, are illuminated intellectually, refined emotionally, and empowered volitionally.

1. CONDUCT IN KEEPING WITH INFORMED INTELLECTS (4:17, 18, 20, 21)

The expression, "the vanity of their mind," in 4:17 could be rendered the aimlessness or resultlessness of their thoughts. Here we have a moronic condition of mind. Note the forceful language used: "darkened," "ignorance," "blindness." We are reminded of Romans 1:28, "And even as they did not like to retain God in their knowledge, God gave them over to a reprobate mind, to do those things which are not convenient." "Reprobate" translates the Greek *adokimos* which literally means unreceptive. Now if a mind is unreceptive it is, as T. R. Glover, late of Cambridge University, once said, "no good." It does not do what a mind is supposed to do.

113

Christians' minds are otherwise than irresponsive and empty to the things of God. Gypsy Smith once related how Ira D. Sankey laid his hand on the gypsy boy's head and prayed that God would make him a preacher. That was in 1876. He continues to proclaim Jesus Christ as Saviour with no thought of retiring though he is in his eighties. God has given him an equipment to stand before kings. And Moody himself, though lacking a formal theological education, had a mind filled with the things of God.

Pursuing this matter of mental equipment further and thinking of its vital relation to conduct, Paul says in verses 20 and 21: "But ye have not so learned Christ; If so be that ye have heard him, and have been taught by him, as the truth is in Jesus." Christians do not "work all uncleanness with greediness." They "have not so learned Christ." It is as though Christ is the essence of what we prize in knowledge. He is our course of study, our curriculum. And when we know Him, we act differently from worldlings. And Paul takes it for granted that professed Christians have been in the school of Christ. Says he, "Ye have heard Him." This is the pupil's part. He must "attend with interest to the lesson to be learned" as the law of the pupil is stated in certain texts on pedagogy. There can be no retention of facts without attention to the lesson to be learned. And the secret of attention is interest. So an interested pupil is attentive; a disinterested pupil is inattentive.

When Jesus' disciples had asked Him why He spoke to the multitudes in parables, He said among other things, "Their ears are dull of hearing . . . But blessed are your eyes, for they see: and your ears, for they hear" (Matt. 13:15,16).

That Jesus' early disciples were keenly interested in His parables is evident from the fact that when He had spoken the parable of the tares they said to Him, "Declare unto us the parable of the tares of the field" (Matt. 13:36). Teaching is at its best when the pupils ask for information from the teacher. Then they are hearing and heeding. They are utilizing their curiosity for the acquisition of useful knowledge.

Let us thank God that we have heard Christ as He spoke through the New Testament writers and as He has spoken to our hearts.

But however eager a pupil may be to learn, his progress is accelerated or retarded according to the efficiency or inefficiency of his teacher. It has been estimated that the teacher counts for eighty-five per cent of the class. Says Paul, "Ye have been taught by Him." Jesus is "The Master Teacher." Measured by the most critical standards of modern pedagogy Jesus' qualifications for teaching are unsurpassed.

> He knew what He taught;
> He knew the world;
> He knew men;
> He knew how to teach;
> He embodied what He taught.

In a broad sense Jesus has influenced more lives than any other teacher. World almanacs report that more than one third of mankind are nominally Christian. This implies that to some degree these millions have learned through Christ even if only the minority are born again believers and earnest students of the Bible.

But our text, "Ye have been taught by him," implies more than nominal discipleship. This we know from the following words, "as the truth is in Jesus." We have learned what He embodied. Recall His words spoken in the Passover room after He had eaten and washed the disciples' feet. Sensing their troubled hearts He comforted them with "Let not your heart be troubled . . . I go to prepare a place for you . . . I will come again, and receive you unto myself." Thomas, given to doubts, said, "Lord, we know not whither thou goest and how can we know the way?" To him Jesus made reply, "I am the way, the truth and the life: no man cometh unto the Father, but by me" (John 14: 5, 6). Did Thomas and the other disciples comprehend what Christ meant? Perhaps not then but probably after Christ had been buried and had risen. He made good His words by His deed. Death could not claim Him as a prey. "In him was life." Certainly He can be followed as our "way." As in the case of the truth of the resurrection to life eternal, so in regard to every truth He spoke, He was the embodiment of that truth.

He spoke of the blessedness of "the poor in spirit" and was content to have "not where to lay His head." He said, "Blessed are they that mourn," and He was "a man of sorrow and acquainted with brief." Further in the beatitudes He advocated meekness, mercy, purity, and peacemaking, and He was "meek and lowly in spirit." He said to the woman taken in adultery, "Neither do I condemn thee; go, and sin no more." He challenged the Pharisees with, "Which of you convinceth me of sin?" And He was acclaimed as "Prince of peace."

Yes, Jesus taught by His life and deeds the very truth He advocated with His lips. He was no hypocrite. He challenges our discipleship with the invitation, "Learn of me."

2. CONDUCT CONGRUOUS WITH REFINED EMOTIONS (4:19)

Of those who walk as other Gentiles walk it can be said, "Who being past feeling have given themselves over unto lasciviousness, to work all uncleanness with greediness." What a sordid picture do these words paint. "Lasciviousness" translates the Greek word, *aselgeia,* whose root meaning may be "not affecting pleasantly." To those who have refined tastes, lustful living is abhorrent. I have just read an article by Velma Hissong entitled "Womanhood—Fortress of Morality." Miss Hissong is no professional writer but an accountant who has taught Sunday school twenty-five years. Her article appeared in St. Louis newspapers, the Christian Advocate, and David C. Cook publications, says *The Protestant Voice,* Nov. 5, 1943. The immediate occasion of her writing was the publishing of a condensed article from *Colliers* in the September number of the *Reader's Digest* under the title of "Husband Shortage." Wrote Miss Hissong, "The Scheinfeld treatment of the problem (since that is what he insists upon calling it) smacks of paganism in pointing out that 'state protection of illegitimacy; sanctioning of sex relationships outside wedlock; a more sexual latitude and even polygamy' are possible solutions." To Miss Hissong the originator of such ideas has "a very poor estimate of the intellectual and spiritual culture of our nation's womanhood."

Another etymology of *aselgeia,* lasciviousness, comes by contrast from a city of Pisidia by the name of *Selge,* whose citizens were very strict morally. In Greek the prefixed *a* gives the negative idea. So those who were given to *aselgeia* were loose morally unlike the good people of Selge.

The terms "being past feeling," "lasciviousness," and "work all uncleanness with greediness" remind us of the character and conduct of the antediluvians who "took them wives of all which they chose" (Gen. 6:2) and so brought on the flood; or of the Canaanites' ill conduct, as reflected in Leviticus 18, where God specifies certain behavior as sinful and says, "for in all these the nations are defiled which I cast out before you," and again, "For all these abominations have the men of the land done, which were before you, and the land is defiled." Or these words remind us of Sodom and Gomorrha, or of that kind of homosexuality described in Romans 1:27 which caused God to give those men over to reprobate minds.

Among the aims of all really great world teachers is that of refining the feelings. And certainly Jesus had this as an aim. The creative artists, the poets, the painters, the musicians, the architects have contributed to lift us out of our matter of fact utilitarian world into an atmosphere where there is no jar, no clash of our loftier sentiments with anything unpleasant. Jesus Christ puts us in tune with the infinite; He transports us into the glorious. The Holy Spirit sublimates our conduct so that we long for and live holy lives and come under the designation of "saints."

Let us listen to the strains of poets of purity of heart and life:

"Lord Jesus, let nothing unholy remain,
Apply thine own blood and extract every stain;
To get this blest cleansing I all things forego—
Now wash me and I shall be whiter than snow."
                                        —J. Nicholson.

"Fountain of purity opened for sin,
Here may the penitent wash and be clean;
Jesus, Thou blessed Redeemer from woe,
Wash me and I shall be whiter than snow."
                                        —Rev. Newmain Hall, D.D.

"Purer, Saviour, purer, May I ever be,
Free from every earth stain,
More, O Lord, like Thee."
                                        —Mrs. C. Warner.

"More holiness give me, more strivings within."
                                        —P. P. Bliss.

"I want the adorning Divine
Thou only, my God, canst bestow;
I want in those beautiful garments to shine,
Which distinguish Thy household below.
I want every moment to feel
That Thy Spirit resides in my heart,
That His power is present to cleanse and to heal,
And newness of life to impart."
                                        —Charlotte Elliott.

3. CONDUCT SPRINGING OUT OF THE WILL (4:22, 23, 24)

As one reads these verses in the Authorized Version he is struck with the fact that the main verb in each verse seems to be an imperative. It is as if the reader is commanded to "Put off . . . the old man"; "Be renewed in the spirit of your mind"; and "Put on the new man." However, a close examination of the Greek text clearly shows us that verses 22, 23, and 24 contain "truth (found) in Jesus."

The Ephesians had "learned Christ." He had been the subject of their course of study. Paul "went into the synagogue and spake boldly for the space of three months." He also was "disputing daily in the school of one Tyrannus . . . by the space of two years" (Acts 19:8-10). Fancy being under the tutelage of Paul and not learning much of Jesus. Just as the presence of light expels the darkness, so Christ and corruption do not belong together. When He went into the temple the money changers had to go out. Christ builds up; the corrupt "old man" would tear down the new creation. Hence we have learned that there must be a putting off of the former manner of life. The same Greek word *apothesthai* is used in I Peter 2:1 where we are admonished to "lay aside all malice . . . guile . . . hypocrisy

. . . envy, and evil speaking." As soiled or worn out garments are unbecoming to those who are being presented at a king's court so "the old man which is corrupting" finds no place in the presence of Christ.

Some years ago the psychologists gave us the expression, "The expulsive power of a new affection." If Christ has our first love we have gone far in ridding ourselves of the old life to which it is natural to cling. As Luke 5:39, thinking of dyed-in-the-wool Pharisaism, says, "No man also having drunk old wine straightway desireth new; for he saith, The old is better." Thus thinks the conservative or reactionary. But Christians are renewed in the spirit of (their) mind, and thus transformed (Rom. 12:2) as is the beautiful monarch butterfly which emerges from the snug cocoon woven by the lowly caterpillar, ground crawler of a former existence.

The worldling looks upon the religious life in a manner entirely different from that of the Christian. He sees through beclouded glasses. We are reminded of those who ask Jesus, "Why do we and the Pharisees fast oft, but thy disciples fast not?" To them Jesus made reply that the presence of the bridegroom makes for joy, not gloom. Then He related two parables to show that old must go with old and new with new. "Neither do men put new wine into old bottles: . . . but they put new wine into new bottles and both are preserved" (Matt. 9:14-17). New in the case of the wine is *neos,* i. e., new in time or recently made; new as used with "bottles" or wine-skins is *kainos,* i. e., new or strong in quality. Christ's new teaching could not be contained by the old, ready to burst, conceptions of Pharisaism, to which the Pharisees held on for dear life. The very spirit of their minds was against their receptivity to the truths of the gospel of the Son of God. So we must have our minds cleansed of old preconceptions and restocked with Christian truth. And thus we put on the new (*kainos,* new kind of a man) man which according to God is created in righteousness and reverence of the truth. And as "other Gentiles" (v. 17) live in unrighteousness and in disregard of truth so our lives become ethical and devoted.

CHAPTER SUMMARY

THE HEAVENLY WALK
(Eph. 4:17-24)

1. Conduct in Keeping with Informed Intellects (vv. 17, 18, 20, 21)
   a. It is not like the aimless living of worldlings (v. 17).
   b. It is unlike the futile living of the ignorant and godless (v. 18; see also Rom. 1:28).
   c. It is patterned after the truth taught and lived by Jesus Christ, who was and is "the truth (v. 20; see John 14:6; 18:37, 38).
   d. Christians have the advantage of being taught by the Master Teacher (v. 21).

2. Conduct Congruous with Refined Emotions (v. 19)
   a. Some "being past feeling" are surrendered to lasciviousness.
   b. The Christian's taste is refined. He aspires to the pure.

3. Conduct Springing Out of the Will (vv. 22, 23, 24)
   These verses contain truth that Jesus taught. They have to do with steps or experiences in the Christian life. They imply the co-operation of the human will reinforced by the Spirit of God.
   a. The old corrupt life must be laid aside (v. 22).
   b. The renewed mind must be filled with high and holy things (v. 23).
   c. The new, holy life must be so lived that the Christian will appear as a new kind of person (v. 24).

Chapter X

SANCTIFIED SPEECH
(Ephesians 4:25-5:14)

A S EPHESIANS 4:1-24 deals in a practical manner with the believer's walk or conduct so 4:25-5:14 deals with our talk or "conversation."

1. ONLY TRUTH SHOULD BE SPOKEN (4:25)

First, we are bidden to put away the practice of lying and speak truth. We observe the contrast between falsehood and truth in that the latter is a statement that conforms to reality or the actual; whereas, falsehood does not match with the facts. The verb "speak," *laleite* in Greek, emphasizes the sounding out of the truth. We are to give expression to truth in dealing with one another since we are all members of the same body and to deceive others is to deceive ourselves eventually and thereby come to grief.

2. THE TEMPER OF THE SPEAKER IS IMPORTANT (4:26, 31, 32)

If we keep in mind the general subject of speaking the exhortation of verse twenty-six takes on a definite meaning. "Be ye angry and sin not" allows for the possibility or probability of anger and assures us that sin need not accompany anger. Uncontrolled anger leads to unwarranted statements. The mind inflamed by rage is ill fitted to express sound judgments.

Our text seems to present a problem in this matter of becoming angry. Verse 26 is stated as a command, "Be ye angry," whereas "wrath" (Greek *thymos,* new or heated anger) and "anger" (Greek *orge,* old or crystallized anger) are listed in 4:31 among those things to be "put away." We are helped in the solution of our problem by observing that "Be ye angry" in verse 26, being in the middle voice, really means intensive or acute anger. The expression suggests being angry for one's own interest. We believe that reference is made here to situations where principles are involved. There are occasions when one should become angry to be true to himself. John B. Gough, noted temperance lecturer of the last century, when but a lad, was walking one day with his sister. A drunken cab driver cracked his whip around the neck of the little girl, whereupon her brother angrily declared himself against the liquor traffic. His sense of right and his love for his sister compelled him to become angry.

The verse continues, "Let not the sun go down upon your wrath," which means that we must not continue in a state of irritation. The setting sun must not see us exasperated. There should be a quick cooling off even if injustice does provoke us. Hence the exhortation of 4:31, "Let all bitterness, and wrath, and anger, and clamor, and evil speaking, be put away from you, with all malice." The climax of all these evils is "malice," which, as F. B. Meyer[1] has said, is "double distilled malignity." This kind of spiteful anger will commit murder.

Prominent in 4:31 are the words, "clamour" and "evil speaking" or blasphemy. Both are types of wrong speaking. Clamour (Gr. *krauge*) refers to harsh instinctive crying out. It implies lack of control and therefore is wrath expressing itself as did Moses when he spake unadvisedly with his lips and called God's children, who had provoked him, "rebels." We who vent our spleen with hasty and heated language should remember that these clamorous words of God's great and honored servant,

[1] F. B. Meyer. *Tried By Fire.*

Moses, kept him out of the Promised Land. A reading of the historical books of the Old Testament impresses us with the goodness of God in permitting us to live in the dispensation of grace, else who would escape? Not only grace but truth came by Jesus Christ. And we are humbled as we face the fact that too often clamour and railing and evil speaking are heard among the saints.

3. SATAN MAY TAKE ADVANTAGE OF OUR TALK (4:27)

"Neither give place to the devil," verse 27, is really a part of verse 26, as the punctuation indicates. And if we are right in concluding that one of the grave evils that may come out of intense anger is unwarranted and harmful speaking, then to "give place to the devil" is to say something that Satan can lay hold of to our disadvantage. Let us beware of our temper as well as be sure of our facts when we speak lest we be compelled to confess as did Job, "Therefore have I uttered that I understood not" (Job 42:3).

Interesting it is that verse 28 should be introduced in this section. It reminds us of James 3:13 in that James 3:1-12 deals with sinning by words or the responsibility of the tongue, and then in verse 13, James seems to leave the subject of the tongue to advise that the wise man will depend upon his "works" rather than his words. Just so here "labour," "working with his own hands" in order to give to him who has a need is a positive way of expressing oneself for good.

4. SPEAK ONLY USEFUL WORDS (4:29)

In 4:29 we have explicit directions as to what not to say as well as what to utter. "Let no corrupt communication proceed out of your mouth," in fairness to the Greek, might well be rendered, "Let each worthless thought not be expressed." *Logos,* translated "communication" in the Authorized Version, means first an idea. A thought may be uttered or unexpressed. If it is "corrupt," (Gr. *sapros*), worthless, why not forget it? As the poet referring to words has sung to children:

> "Keep them back if they're cold and cruel,
> Under bar and lock and seal,
> For the wounds that they make, my darlings,
> Are always slow to heal."

"But," continues 4:29, "that which is good to the use of edifying, that it may minister grace unto the hearers." This means that a good word which builds up should be uttered. The test is as to whether or not it supplies the need or satisfies the hearers. When Jesus had spoken in His own Nazareth synagogue (Luke 4:16-21) all were testifying to Him and were marveling at the words of grace which proceeded out from His mouth and kept saying, "Is not this one a son of Joseph?" Their question implies that they are surprised at one of their own townspeople speaking such words of grace. As Proverbs 25:11 says, "A word fitly spoken is like apples of gold in pictures of silver." As golden colored apples blend with a frame of silver so should a word fit into a needy situation.

5. UNHOLY SPEECH GRIEVES THE SPIRIT (4:30)

"And grieve not the holy Spirit of God, whereby ye are sealed unto the day of redemption" (4:30), is a passage worthy of being lifted out of its context and used as an exhortation. But why not accept it as a part of our segment on speaking and consider that we grieve the Holy Spirit by unholy speech? To "grieve" is to cause to be sad or sorrowful. And to bring grief to the Spirit of God by our evil speaking is to behave like ingrates since He has "sealed (us) unto redemption day." According to 1:13, "After that ye believed, ye were sealed with that holy Spirit of promise." He met our faith with the securing seal of the Godhead and assured us of all the blessings of eternal salvation.

6. OUT OF THE HEART THE MOUTH SPEAKS (4:31-5:4)

We have already alluded to 4:31, but it is in place here to note that "evil speaking" is a translation of *blasphemia* which, literally, means stupid speech. And note the company kept by such speech. Those who are "bitter" and wrathful and malicious are apt to raise their voices in stupid expressions. So did the poet Hipponax, born at Ephesus, whose caustic words gave him the name of *Ho Pikros,* "the Bitter." He even spoke disparagingly of marriage, but Paul uses this holy state to teach spiritual truth. But what is the corrective for this bitterness? We find the specific for the malady in 4:32 and 5:1, 2. We are urged to be "kind." The Greek *chrestoi* which is rendered "kind" means fit for use. A jar of wine which was ready to be drunk with complete satisfaction was *chrestos* and kindness deals with our fellows as kindred or kin. We are instructed further by "tenderhearted" and "forgiving" as associates or explanations of what "kind" implies. Rather than rail at our enemies we must forgive them "even as God for Christ's sake hath forgiven." And thus we will realize that "perfection" of which our Lord speaks in Matthew 5:48 which goes with carrying out His command to "Bless them that curse you" (Matthew 5:44).

What a challenge to exemplary conduct is set forth in "Be ye therefore followers of God, as dear children" (5:1). "Followers of God" are those who imitate God. He forgives because Christ died for us and so paid the penalty for our sins. "Therefore" as His beloved children we should forgive rather than call names.

Thus we "walk in love," or as the present tense of the verb suggests "continue to walk in love." And this we should do rather than "name" certain unmentionable types of conduct whose very description is defiling. "As becometh saints," ones separated from these evil practices, we do well to exclude speech regarding "fornification, and all uncleanness, or covetousness." Along with these are classed "filthiness" or obscenity, and "foolish talking." Commenting on the latter, Archbishop Trench, author of Synonyms of the N.T., writes, "Discourse not seasoned with the salt of grace. Foolishness and sin go together, disclosing the hidden man of the heart." Some one has put it thus: "Filthiness," *aischrotes* is foulness; *morologia* is foolishness; and "jesting," *eytrapelia,* is false refinement in speaking.

7. "JESTING" DEFINED (5:4)

Of all three words it is said, "which are not convenient" or becoming. "Jesting" translates the Greek *eytrapelia* which literally means easily or readily turning and refers to nimble wit. It is a term which suggests false refinement in speaking, a sprinkling of perfume over the garbage can. Paul recommends "giving of thanks" rather than foolish talking or jesting. In doing so he plays upon two Greek words very much alike in appearance and sound but very unlike in what they signify. He disapproves of *eytrapelia* but approves of *eycharistia.* The root idea in the latter word is to "satisfy well" and reminds us of Paul's admonition, "Let your speech be alway with grace, seasoned with salt" (Col. 4:6a). Well seasoned speech smacks of good sense or sound judgment. It satisfies. And thus does the language used by one of a grateful heart. "Giving of thanks" to our friends for what they contribute to our lives and to God for His gifts, "good and perfect," this is becoming to a Christian. The "vain words" mentioned in 5:6 are those void of any content that is satisfactory to a

Christian. They originate with those designated in 5:5 as "whoremonger . . . unclean person nor covetous man, who is an idolator." These are all "children of disobedience" upon whom "cometh the wrath of God" as 5:6 says. Their speech is just as empty as their lives are void of good.

Hence 5:7 advises, "Be not ye therefore partakers with them." God's Word advocates separation from sinners. This vile world is no friend to grace to help us on to God. The associations of Sodom contaminated Lot's family. The New Testament calls Christians "saints" or separated ones. To the Israelites in Canaan the Lord commanded, "Defile not ye yourselves in any of these things: for in all these the nations are defiled which I cast out before you." Then Jehovah explains, "and the land is defiled: therefore I do visit the iniquity thereof upon it, and the land itself vomiteth out her inhabitants" (Lev. 18:24, 25). What a figure! Why this vomiting? It was caused mostly by the sexual sins of the Canaanites as Leviticus 18 describes—adultery, sodomy, and such sins. Society today is being corrupted by immorality. Let us beware of both the dark deeds and the foul words of libertines. We must "walk as children of light" (5:8), unafraid of the sunlight of the day. Says Eadie,[2] "The Ephesians had prided themselves in Alexander, the philosopher, and they fondly surnamed him the 'Light'; but his teaching had left the city in such gloom that the apostle was obliged to say to them, 'Ye were sometimes darkness'; and himself was the first unshaded luminary that rose on that benighted province." And Paul, like we, but reflected Him who was "The True Light."

Christianity provides an experience as well as a body of teaching. There is a "Christian experience" for each child of God. You may test out the teachings of the Bible, as myriads have done, and then give your own testimony as to your findings. Hence

---

[2] John Eadie, *Commentary on the Greek Text of the Epistle of Paul to the Ephesians,*

5:10 says "Proving what is acceptable unto the Lord." But Paul is so sure that those who "try" the Christian way will find it acceptable that what he really says is "approving by testing (*dokimazo* in Greek) what is well pleasing to the Lord."

8. ELOQUENT LIVING (5:11)

But whereas we are to prove and then approve God's good pleasure, we are admonished to "reprove" the unfruitful works of darkness, 5:11. This means, as the original text instructs us, to convince as well as convict those who do evil. This can best be done by the eloquence of holy living rather than by lives of compromise. "Have no fellowship" with them says verse 11. Be not partners with sinners but be expressive against sin. Speak by lip and life against all that will not stand the test of truth.

When former President Woodrow Wilson was a professor at Princeton University he had occasion to be in Chicago. One day he was being shaved in a barber shop when suddenly the door of the shop opened and forthwith the conversation changed. "Who came in?" asked Wilson. "An evangelist by the name of Moody," was the barber's reply.

CHAPTER SUMMARY

SANCTIFIED SPEECH
(Eph. 4:25-5:14)

Though much of the material found in this segment pertains to conduct rather than conversation, as we use this word today, yet we prefer to utilize all of it to emphasize the importance of proper speech among Christians.

1. Only Truth Should Be Spoken (4:25)
2. The Temper of the Speaker Is Important (4:26, 31, 32)
   a. There is a form of anger, sometimes called "righteous indignation," which is not sinful (v. 26a).

    b. A Christian should not continue in a state of irritation (v. 26b).

    c. Anger and its accompaniments which lead to loud or blasphemous talk should be put away (v. 31).

    d. Kindness is Christlike and makes for proper talk (v. 32).

3. Satan May Take Advantage of Our Talk (4:27)

4. Speak Only Useful Words (4:29)

5. Unholy Speech Grieves the Spirit (4:30)

6. Out of the Heart the Mouth Speaks (4:31-5:4)

7. Jesting Defined (5:4)

    a. It is false refinement in discourse.

    b. It is the opposite of thanksgiving.

8. Eloquent Living (5:11)

The holy life speaks so clearly and convincingly that it condemns the ungodly words and deeds of sinners.

Chapter XI

WALKING CAREFULLY
(Ephesians 5:15-6:9)

CHRISTIANS should be exact in their own walk rather than exacting of others. Of Dr. A. B. Simpson and a saintly Italian brother, Mr. Nardi, the late Dr. Agide Pirazzini, professor of Hebrew at Biblical Seminary, said: "They were real saints. They were severe with themselves and generous with others; whereas, most saints are generous with themselves and severe with others." The "wise" recognize values. They are thorough going. "Fools" are careless and care free. Wisdom appreciates the worth of opportunity as "redeeming the time" (5:16) suggests. The picture presented in this portion is that of a market where goods are purchased. The meaning is, "buying back (at the expense of personal watchfulness and self-denial) the present time, which is now being used for evil and godless purposes"—Moulton and Milligan. "Time" in verse sixteen is from the Greek, *kairos,* which means a certain period, season, or point of time. We have the idea in the expression, "psychological moment."

Christians should make use of each opportunity to represent Christ "because the days are evil." Says Matthew Henry, "Those were times of persecution wherein the apostle wrote this: the Christians were in jeopardy every hour." But are not we living in evil days? Young men by the millions are on the march to the battle front. This is their hour to accept Christ. Realizing imminent physical danger many of them are coming to Christ. We should see to it that they know the "way."

The exhortations of verses 14, 15, and 16 are urgent. They exist because of unfavorable conditions about which something should be done. Hence the "wherefore be ye not unwise but understanding what the will of the Lord is" of verse seventeen. "Unwise," *aphrones,* literally rendered, means not using one's head or mind. "Understanding," *syniete,* means sending or putting together. The thoughtful Christian places the life of his day alongside of "the will of the Lord" as revealed in His Word and judges accordingly. He is no superficial optimist nor is he a despairing pessimist but a confirmed Biblicist. The Bible is his "rule of faith and practice." He regards its admonitions and embraces its promises. In reverent prayer he utters, "Thy will be done."

"And be not drunk with wine, wherein is excess; but be filled with the Spirit" of verse eighteen goes with verse seventeen. Indeed the "unwise" get drunk with wine but the "understanding" are "filled with (the Holy) Spirit."

When men are drunk "with wine" they go to "excess," (Greek, *asotia*) i. e., literally, they are not "saving." The prodigal son "wasted his substance in riotous (*asotos*) living," i. e., he did not save but squandered with reckless prodigality. His life was careless. His was the excitement of suddenly acquired wealth, and consequently his life was not regulated.

But those "filled with the Spirit" live within a certain pattern. Their expressions are inclusive of all that is becoming to a Christian. They sing "psalms," accompanied by a musical instrument, "hymns," praises to God, and "spiritual songs" in general.

In fact there are presented here three characteristics of the spirit-filled Christian which make for his circumspect walk: spiritual singing, spontaneous thanksgiving, and submissive living.

1. SPIRITUAL SINGING (5:18, 19)

Some one has said, "Let me write the songs of a nation and I care not who makes her laws." This means that our songs affect our conduct more than do our laws. And songs reflect the soul of a people. Each war period produces its own songs if the war is one into which the people's emotions enter. Commentators observe that World War II has not yet given rise to any new songs but the boys sing old songs. College campuses have their songs. National anthems stir the soul. Great revivals of religion produce or utilize suitable hymns. And the sweet singers fill out the picture. John Wesley preached and Charles sang. Sankey's singing of "The Ninety and Nine" and such hymns went with Moody's world stirring messages. Chapman had his Alexander and Sunday his Rodeheaver. And Dr. A. B. Simpson's hymns were a by-product of his preaching. The major strain of the Christian hymn has carried the doctrine of saving faith to the lost of each age since the multitude of the heavenly host sang to the wondering shepherds, "Glory to God in the highest, and on earth peace, good will to men."

We note that of the Spirit-filled Christians it is said, "Speaking to yourselves in psalms and hymns and spiritual songs, singing and making melody in your heart to the Lord." We edify, exhort, encourage, and enlighten ourselves by congregational singing of the psalms of divine inspiration and the spiritual songs of divine illumination. We unitedly praise God through the great hymns of the church. These provide words and tunes which wing our deepest devotion and most intimate yearning in grand concert to the ears of the Lord of hosts.

Such melody is made in the heart. Mere vocalizing ill becomes a Christian. Spirit-filled souls care more for the sense and the sentiment than for the sound. The melody is from the heart "to the Lord." Such singing goes with and begets careful conduct.

2. SPONTANEOUS THANKSGIVING (5:18, 19)

We have referred to the second characteristic of a Spirit-filled Christian as spontaneous thanksgiving because if it were otherwise it could not be "always for all things." The late Dr. Troy, a Brooklyn pastor, related an unforgettable incident of his life when the writer was a babe in Christ. He was far from home when word came of the serious illness of his child. As he waited for his train he was pacing the platform restlessly. There flashed through his brain Paul's words to the Thessalonians, "In everything give thanks: for this is the will of God in Christ Jesus concerning you" (I Thess. 5:18). Immediately this servant of the Lord lifted his heart in thanksgiving to his Father in heaven and the peace of God flooded his soul.

Contrast this attitude of the Spirit-filled life with the thanklessness of our day. Says Paul, "In the last days . . . men shall be . . . unthankful, unholy" (II Tim. 3:1, 2). The Holy Spirit makes us thankful. The unholy are also unthankful. Thank is akin to think. The thankless are thoughtless.

Eycharistountes, "Giving thanks," is composed of *ey,* well, and the same root as *charis,* grace; hence being well graced, gracious or grateful. And this root has the idea of satisfactory. So thankfulness is from the heart that is satisfied. It is also satisfying to the one thanked. How God must be pleased when we thank Him for His great goodness.

3. SUBMISSIVE LIVING (5:18-6:9)

The third manifestation of the Spirit-filled life is submissive living. "Submitting yourselves one to another in fear of God," (5:21) is a topic sentence for the section 5:22-6:9.

Here we have concrete reciprocal relations that have to do with domestic life. These are the marriage relationship (5:22-33), the parent and child relationship (6:1-4) and that between master and servant (6:5-9).

In the case of the first of these we find much that is mutual between husband and wife even though a superficial reader might interpret the passage as teaching that the husband is lord of the wife. True it is that she should "submit" to her own husband. And it is just as evident that he should "love" her. These terms and their context bear our close study.

"Submit" translates *hypotasso* in the middle voice. The meaning is to order oneself under. Hence submission calls for the exercise of the will. The wife obeys rather than has her own way. And this she does with a will even though her nature might make it impossible for her to do this willingly. As wrote Longfellow in Hiawatha's Wooing:

> "As unto the bow the cord is
> So unto the man is woman;
> Though she bends she obeys him;
> Though she draws him yet she follows:
> Useless each without the other."

So the strong minded woman may become an ideal wife. "As unto the Lord" can be understood best by continuing with verse 23, "For the husband is the head of the wife, even as Christ is the head of the church." Mark the analogy. The wife, as a wife, is related to her husband as is the church to Christ. Manifestly the church must be submissive to Christ, the Head, and likewise a wife must submit to her own husband. And verse fourteen adds "in everything." And upon this the Expositor's Greek Testament comments "in everything that pertains to marriage." This same work interprets "as unto the Lord" in verse 22 as meaning that the wife should "obey her husband as she obeys Christ." But in the case of the relationship between Christ and the church it is said, "He is the saviour of the body." The body is the church which Christ died to save. This could not be said of the husband. And if obedience on the part of the wife is expected in the very nature of things how much more should the church be expected implicitly to obey Christ, the heavenly Bridegroom.

Now if this Pauline presentation of the woman's position in the marital state seems out of keeping with the ideal marriage conception of our day, let us suspend judgment until we canvass Paul's demands upon the husband. Wrote he, "Husbands, love your wives, even as Christ also loved the church, and gave himself for it" (5:25). Wrote F. B. Meyer: "Chrysostom says: 'Wouldest thou that thy wife obey thee as the Church doth Christ? Have care for her, then, as Christ for the Church.' Our earthly relationships are similitudes and emblems of sacred realities, and the more we can import into the time sphere the inspiration and virtue of the eternal, the more transcendental and beautiful will they become."

"Love" in 5:25 is *agapao*. The Greek language is rich in its synonyms for "love." *Agape* means unselfish altruistic concern for another's good. *Filia* carries the idea of liking the one loved. *Stergo* is used to speak of a parent's affection for a child. *Eros* means sexual passion. This brief study enables us to see that a husband is expected to have in mind his wife's good and happiness. This is made clear as we read, "even as Christ loved the church and gave himself for it." "For" here translates *hyper* which carries the idea of substitution. Hence we have an allusion to Christ crucified in our stead, dying that we might live. Such in principle is the love a man should have for the woman who has become his wife.

In the case of Christ the aim of His loving sacrificial death was the sanctification and glorification of the church. "Sanctify" translates *hagiazo,* which means separate. So Christ would have His church separated from the defilements of the world unto Himself to be in reverence and holiness. "Glorious" (5:27), *endoxon,* means illustrious or notable. Christ would have the church, His bride, attractively beautiful in that she is free from "spot," *spilon,* an external spot, and "blemish," *rhytida,* an internal blemish. "So, (*houtos,* in this manner) ought men to love their wives as their own bodies." Verse 31 says, "and they two shall be one flesh." This physical oneness implies a mystical union, which is dissolved only by death.

Christ's sanctifying of the church was in order to "present it to himself a glorious church." The husband's loving care for his wife will make for himself a life partner who will reflect credit upon him. Her happiness and good deeds will speak to the world of his generosity and thoughtfulness on her behalf. And she should reciprocate in kind so that "Her husband is known in the gates, when he sitteth among the elders of the land" (Prov. 31:23). So in Ephesians 5:22-33 we have marriage sublimated. Realizing that his analogy has been carried far, Paul says, "This is a great mystery: but I speak concerning Christ and the church" (5:32). This is as though the real spiritual relationship that exists between Christ and His body, the church, may find its earthly counterpart in marriage, which may be conceived of as a parable of the union of Christ and His bride, the church. And Spirit-filled husbands and wives are capable of such mountain top marriage felicity.

But some one may ask, what if either party to the contract fails? The writer knew of such a case. The wife came miserably short of being a meek, submissive, respectful spouse. But her groom constantly carried out the principles of Scripture and won the renown of sainthood among those who knew. And has not Christ's love been spurned all too often, though He tasted death for every man?

Continuing the thought of "submitting yourselves one to another in the fear of God," Paul introduces to us the subject of the relationship of children and parents. He bids children to "obey" parents in the Lord. *Hypakouo,* "obey," literally, means to hear under. It implies to hearken or heed. "For this is right," says the Apostle. "Right" translates *dikaion,* which is connected in root with *deiknymi,* to show. Hence the "right" is that which should obtain according to the constitution of things as they are evident to all who have eyes to see. So Paul means to say, "Obviously, children should obey their parents."

But some modern educators have been so fearful of parents and teachers taking advantage of children that they have advocated the "free reign" theory. It is related that John Dewey was once standing by a mud puddle in which his son, recently garbed in a clean suit, was splashing about. Whereupon a friend called, "John, what are you thinking about?" To which the famous philosopher made reply, "I am trying to conceive of a suggestion to bring him out of that mud without actually commanding him." This theory bids us not to cross the child's will lest we hinder his development. "Self expression" is regarded as of paramount value.

But the thoughtful see in our present crime wave the harvest of such sowing. We have sown the wind and are now reaping the whirlwind. Boy delinquents are up 11% and girls 38% as compared to 1940. J. Edgar Hoover of F.B.I. is "shocked and alarmed" and calls upon the home and Sunday school to come to the rescue. Writers who believe in "spare the rod and spoil the child," are recommending a return to the "woodshed remedy."

Coupled with the admonition to "obey" is that to "honor" parents (6:2). The Greek of this is *tima,* to value or estimate and hence to honor. And Paul reminds us that this is "the first commandment with promise." And the promise is two-fold: success and longevity. "Well" of 6:3 is *ey* in Greek. These two letters so combined are worn on the lapel of the coat by some Greeks as a token of good luck much as some people carry charms to insure "good luck." In his autobiography, Charles H. Spurgeon tells of his call to preach before he had gone far in his education work.

His father desired him to take a formal course but Charles, then a young preacher, longed to continue to proclaim the good news of salvation and do his studies under a tutor. This he submitted to his father by letter and deferred to paternal decision on the matter so vital to himself. Certainly Spurgeon succeeded and his influence goes on and on. He does "live long."

But if children are to "obey" and "honour," Christian parents have their solemn obligations also. "Ye fathers, provoke not your children to wrath: but bring them up in the nurture and admonition of the Lord" (6:4). Here four Greek words of importance clamor for attention. *Parorgizete* means irritate. The noun form is in 4:26. Parents may be a source of irritation to children. Some fathers are sandpaper. They should glove the hand before they touch the child. So we see that although we may properly refer to "Pauline discipline," yet we must observe that Paul is no inhuman disciplinarian. He reminds us of the preacher of our acquaintance who kissed his flaxen haired little girl and wept before he chastised her. "Bring them up," *ektrefete,* is primarily nourish or more literally still, feed out. Farmers in the middle west buy cattle from the far western ranges and place them in feeding lots where they are nourished and marketed as "corn fed" stock. The kind of mental and spiritual provisions furnished by fathers for their children figure largely in their futures. "Nurture," *paideia,* suggests the physical punishment that a parent may inflict upon a child as well as "the whole training and education of children" (Thayer). "Admonition," *nouthesia,* composed of *nous,* mind, and *tithemi,* place, means to place upon the mind and refers to impressions made by the use of words either of encouragement or remonstrance. Thus we see that the duties of a Spirit-filled parent are marked out. He is no despotic tyrant nor is he an over indulgent grandfather. And his work is so highly esteemed that even his children grown to maturity will give him reverence (Heb. 12:9).

The third reciprocal relationship dealt with in this connection is that of masters and servants. Although the institution of slavery has been non-existent in America since 1863, yet there are principles set forth in this Scripture that we do well to observe. We might see an analogy here that will apply to employees and their employers.

It is evident that the institution of slavery was accepted as a fact and neither approved nor disapproved by Paul. His attitude toward property rights as well as human liberty can be seen by a study of his epistle to Philemon.

Upon the slaves (*douloi,* bond servants) the apostle enjoined genuine obedience to their masters. When he admonishes them to serve "with fear and trembling" he is calling for that same "solicitous zeal" which he exhibited in his own ministry (I Cor. 2:3) and for which he calls in the Corinthians (II Cor. 7:15) and the Philippians (Phil. 2:12). Are they servants, then they should serve in reality "in singleness of . . . heart, as unto Christ." "Singleness" translates *haplotes* which, etymologically, means without folds, and hence without duplicity. "Masters," *kyrioi,* were the owners of their servants in that day and consistency demanded faithful service. By the same line of reasoning employees, or "hired men," owe genuine service for which they are paid. Anything other than this is termed "eyeservice" and those who render it are called "men pleasers." But such standards as these words imply are far beneath the dignity and duty of the Christian who should be sincere in his service and should in all he does be "doing the will of God from the heart." "Heart" here translates *psyche,* soul, which is the seat of personality or the inner self. Workers should put themselves into their work as if laboring for the Lord whose eyes are never closed. All should be done in "good will" (Eph. 6:5-7). Both bond and free, employee and employer, will be dealt with fairly by the Judge of all. Souls will come before the judgment seat of Christ as souls;

not attired as lords and ladies on the one hand, or servants and handmaidens on the other. Kings and paupers will be dealt with and rewarded as individuals.

And therefore to the "masters" Paul says "forbear," *anientes,* or omit threatening. As the servants should be real so should the masters. Their word ought to be a true word. And as Spirit-filled Christians they must reckon with their "Master." Nestle's Greek text has it *kai anton kai hymon ho Kyrios,* i. e., both their and your Lord or Master. The same Lord who owns the servants also possesses the masters. Both have to do with Him, who is "in heaven." And, continues the verse, *prosopolempsia,* face receiving, is not with Him. If the masters attempt to conceal their true heart attitude with the mask of a hypocritical face they are due to disillusionment. He looks upon the heart and so judges.

CHAPTER SUMMARY

WALKING CAREFULLY
(Eph. 5:15-6:9)

1. Spiritual Singing (5:18, 19)
   a. The Christian's singing should contain "psalms and hymns and spiritual songs."
   b. It should be from the heart to the Lord.

2. Spontaneous Thanksgiving (5:18, 20)
   a. We should always be thankful.
   b. We should "give thanks . . . for all things."
   c. God the Father should receive our thanks "in the name of our Lord Jesus Christ."

3. Submissive Living (5:18, 21-6:9)
   Under this head we study particular reciprocal relations.
   a. That of husband and wife (5:21-33).
      (1) The husband is the head of the wife as Christ is the Head of the Church (v. 23).

(2) Wives should be subject to their own husbands (v. 24).

(3) Husbands should love their wives as Christ loved the Church (v. 25).

(4) Such love is altruistic and profitable (vv. 26-30).

(5) The husband should sacrifice all for his wife since they are one (v. 31).

(6) The marriage relationship is sublime and symbolic (v. 32).

(7) Love and reverence should characterize marriage (v. 33).

b. The relationship of parents and children (6:1-4)

(1) Obedience is "right" (v. 1).

(2) "Honor" of parents is a commandment (v. 2a).

(3) To obey parents is to keep this "commandment with promise" (vv. 2b, 3).

(4) Parents must not "provoke" their children (v. 4a).

(5) Parents should train their children (v. 4b).

c. The relationship of masters and servants (6:5-9)

(1) Servants should obey conscientiously (vv. 5, 6).

(2) "Eye service" is condemned (vv. 5, 6).

(3) Ideal service is voluntary (v. 7).

(4) The Lord rewards faithful service (v. 8).

(5) God holds masters responsible for their conduct to their servants (v. 9).

CHAPTER XII

FACING THE FOE
(Ephesians 6:10-20)

FINALLY, my brethren, be strong in the Lord, and in the power of his might" not only introduces us to the conclusion of this letter but to its hortatory climax. We sense an unusual urgency here. There is need of strength as we face this foe. As Martin Luther sang:

> "For still our ancient foe
> Doth seek to work us woe;
> His craft and power are great,
> And armed with cruel hate
> On earth is not his equal.

> "Did we in our own strength confide,
> Our striving would be losing:
> Were not the right man on our side,
> The Man of God's own choosing."

We are exhorted to "be strong" (6:10), *endynamousthe,* manifestly strong, in the Lord even by means of the power, *kratei* (6:10), applied power, of His might, *ischyos* (6:10), endowed strength as an elephant has it. So Paul desires to see believers manifesting the might of the Lord as it is applied in their daily practice. This might is available to us. Why not be strong?

1. THE STRENGTH OF OUR FOE (6:11, 12)

And preparation for a fight with this foe calls for a protective defense as well as positive offensive equipment. Hence we must have "the whole armour," *panoplian,* (6:11) of God in order to stand against the "wiles," *methodias,* methods, deceits, pretentions of the devil. And the Greek *methodias* is composed of *meta,* after and *hodos,* a way. A "method" is the course or way one takes after trial or investigation. And Satan has had experience in the art of deceit. Hence his deceits are really deceptive. Satan's "wiles" are like a prize fighter's "feints." The pugilist pretends to hit you with one fist while he is waiting for a surprise blow with the other. The soul's enemy would strike where least expected. He is "the devil," *tou diabolou,* (6:11), the one who opposes by throwing a hindrance across your path. So "we wrestle not against flesh and blood," mere human nature—that would be comparatively easy—but against "principalities," *archas,* (those who have the *first* place or power); against "powers," *exousias,* authorities, against "the rulers of the darkness" (6:12), *kosmokratoras tou skotous toutou,* literally, world rulers of this darkness. *Kosmokrator,* "world ruler," according to the Orphic Hymns, means Satan; according to Gnostic writings the term means the devil. But he dominates only "this darkness" of the ignorant world as it now is. His rule will be cut short in due time.

The exhortation of 6:11 is repeated in 6:13. Twice we are urged to put on "the whole armour of God." But in the second instance we have a "wherefore," *dia touto,* on account of this set of circumstances. Since the devil is wily, since we must contend against a formidable array of wicked spiritual forces; therefore, we need the protective covering which God has provided. This will enable us to "withstand," *antistenai,* (6:13) stand against the forces of evil which we are bound to face and "having done all," *katergasamenoc* (6:13) have wrought intensively, or fought valiantly, "to stand," *stenai,* maintain our position.

"How well Horatius kept the bridge,
   In the brave days of old";

These lines remind us of one who did exploits by standing in the face of danger. There were many other men in that company, but only Horatius held the bridge that spanned the Tiber in 508 B.C.

2. "THE WHOLE ARMOUR OF GOD"

a. THE GIRDLE OF TRUTH (6:14a).

"Stand . . . having your loins girt about with truth" pictures for us one who is every inch a soldier of the Cross. The girdle kept the other parts of the armour in place and secured a proper soldierly attitude and freedom of movement. Ellicott[2] says that "truth" here means candor and sincerity. What an asset to any Christian is sincerity. Can we conceive of an insincere Christian? Christ Himself was "the Truth." As the girdle encompasses the soldier so let truth be round about us so that our "word is as good as our note." Then as Dr. H. H. Horne[3] says, "Truth is harmony between idea and fact." If our ideas are true they will work. So just as an athlete is free to move about if his loins are girt with a girdle, so are we free if truth is the girdle of the loins of our mind (I Pet. 1:13). Said Jesus, "Ye shall know the truth, and the truth shall make you free" (John 8:32). Ultimate victory is assured every Christian soldier because his principles are sound. In the days of Julian, the apostate, the Christians were having a hard time because of persecutions. One day Libanius, the celebrated rhetorician, tauntingly asked a simple hearted Christian of Antioch, "What is your carpenter doing now?" To

---

[2] C. J. Ellicott. *Critical and Grammatical Commentary on Ephesians.*
[3] H. H. Horne. *The Philosophy of Education.* (MacMillan, New York, 1909).

which the Christian made apt reply, "He is making a coffin for the emperor." And ere Julian died he cried out, "Galilean, thou hast conquered." Christ always conquers. He is the Truth. He came to testify to the truth.

> "Truth crushed to earth will rise again;
> The eternal years of God are hers.
> But error, wounded, writhes in pain
> And dies among his worshippers."
>
> —Bryant.

b. The Breastplate of Righteousness (6:14b).

This is covering for the vital organs, the seat of the emotions. "Of righteousness" is a genitive of apposition and so the expression means righteousness as a breastplate. The Greek term for righteousness is *dikaiosyne,* which signifies what ought to be. Hence "moral rectitude" is implied. In the case of Bible Christians there is an objective standard upon which our ethics is based. We accept the moral standards of the New Testament as final and in force for us. We believe that much of the immorality of our times is due to the fact that unbelief has robbed youth of their confidence in the Bible as "a rule of faith and practice."

When Zaccheus, the publican, met Jesus he said, "Behold, Lord, the half of my goods I give to the poor; and if I have taken any thing from any man by false accusation, I restore him fourfold." Jesus, recognizing a truly penitent believer said, "This day is salvation come to this house . . . For the Son of man is come to seek and to save that which was lost" (Luke 19:8-10). Those who meet Jesus and call him "Lord," *kyrie,* owner, ruler, will set their houses in order. To be a Christian is to be ethical. Only the pseudo-Christian is ever called a "hypocrite." Christians are expected to be righteous. This is the greatest compliment that could be paid to Christ and Christianity. Only the righteous can "stand."

C. THE SHOES OF THE GOSPEL (6:15).

In World War I there was the "Pershing shoe" which guaranteed foot ease to the American soldier. The hymn writer has pictured the sinner as

> "Foot-sore, lame and weary,
> Your garments stained with sin."

We who contend with or stand against "spiritual wickedness in high places" must have our "feet shod with the preparation of the gospel of peace" (6:15). A telling word here is "preparation," *hetiomasia,* readiness or "promptitude and alacrity" (Thayer). Those who believe the gospel are swift to obey the Lord. As Dr. A. B. Simpson has written:

> "Press on my heart the woe;
> Put in my feet the go;
> Let me be faithful to my trust
> And use me for thy glory."

In Romans 10:15 Paul raises the question, "and how shall they preach, except they be sent?" Then quoting Isaiah he says in beautiful prose, "How beautiful are the feet of them that preach the gospel of peace." In this verse "beautiful" is a translation of *horaioi* which means suitable to the season, seasonable, or timely. Then it came to be used to refer to the prime of life, youth, or the beauty of youth. So "beautiful feet" are feet that approach the sinner when he is needing a Saviour. The foot-fall of the evangelist is music to the ear of the penitent, as is the coming of a trusted physician or the healing touch of the Great Physician to him who is languishing in pain. What a firm stand against the kingdom of evil does the preacher of peace make.

d. THE SHIELD OF FAITH (6:16).

This shield was quite large and shaped like a door. Hence the name in Greek *thyreon,* from *thyra,* door. Its size and shape enabled it to protect the whole body of the soldier. So faith shields the Christian. Confidence in Christ displaces fear. "Of faith" is a genitive of apposition and so our expression means Faith as a Shield. "Taking," *analabontes,* literally means taking up. It is as though the Christian should consciously pick up his faith in Christ when danger approaches. For with faith as a shield "ye shall be able to quench all the fiery darts of the wicked." And "the wicked one" hurls darts dipped in doubt, fired in hell. And the perfect participle *pepyromena* (6:16) means that the arrow was brought to a glowing heat and continues to remain full of fire. It may be that the arrow referred to was combustible and burnt more brightly the swifter it flew and thus would set on fire a wooden shield, or the dart could have been poisoned and so would cause a burning sensation in the wound, but in either case a protective shield would "quench" its effects.

Since faith is positive rather than negative this part of the armour has been called "an offensive defense." Some prizefighters rely upon their own swift punches to hold off their opponents. And we depend upon Christ, our Champion, to defeat Satan. He "spoiled principalities and powers . . . triumphing over them in it (the cross)" (Col. 2:15). And just as the shield is "above all," i. e., over all as *epi* suggests, so faith is our topmost weapon of defense. We say "I suppose" for the sake of argument; and "I think" when we have a degree of confidence; and "I believe" when we have come to a state of mental rest; and "I know" when we have reached the highest degree of certainty. But, philosophically, when we really believe, we have been persuaded subjectively and this is assurance enough. So faith is ultimate and serves as knowledge. We "believers" can hear Jesus say to us as

He did to the sinful, yet believing woman, opposed by Simon the Pharisee, "Thy faith hath saved thee; go in peace" (Luke 7:50).

e. The Helmet of Salvation (6:17).

We are urged to "receive the helmet of salvation." "Take" of the Authorized Version is a translation of the Greek *dechomai* which ordinarily means passive receptivity, rather than active appropriation. The exhortation is to regard salvation as a covering for the head as *perikephalaion,* "helmet," means. In I Thessalonians 5:8, where Paul is writing to those troubled doctrinally regarding the Lord's return, he urges "Putting on . . . for an helmet, the hope of salvation." A knowledge of salvation provides a solution to many problems. If the heart is right with God the thinking usually straightens out.

How important that adolescents, young people, have the experience of salvation from sin through faith in Jesus Christ. At that age there is a proneness to question. The credulity of childhood passes through the criticism of adolescence before it arrives at the conviction of maturity. During later adolescence, young people are being tested mentally in the schools. Our system of grading over-emphasizes intellectual attainment and so the youth cannot be blamed for submitting everything to the test of his reason. He rings the changes on "Come let us reason together," but alas, all too often, he fails to connect this Scripture with having the scarlet and the crimson of his record made white as snow by being washed in the blood of the Lamb.

A great preacher once said that while attending a university as a young man, his faith was severely tested. But, although he could not "always give an answer to every man that asked him a reason of the hope that was in him," yet he never got away from the fact of his boyhood experience of salvation. Certain knowledge of sins forgiven, salvation from sins committed in the past,

aided him to think scripturally as he sought for solution to his
religious problems.

Recall the healing by Jesus of the man born blind, as John 9
records. When the Pharisees attempted to get him to renounce
Jesus, who had given him sight, he said, "One thing I know,
that, whereas I was blind, now I see." This knowledge, as a
starting point, enabled him to make such a defense of his faith in
Jesus that the Pharisees could not successfully contradict him. So
"they cast him out." But Jesus took him in. "And he worshipped him." Such a Saviour as Jesus would be God as well as
man; He would rise from the dead; He would work wonders;
He would prophesy and predict. I claim Him as my Prophet,
Priest, and King.

f. The Sword of the Spirit (6:17b).

We are not left to our own interpretation as to what is meant
here. "The sword of the Spirit, which is the word of God," goes
with "The helmet of salvation."

In the eleventh chapter of Isaiah we have a picture of the
righteous rule and millennial glory of Christ's kingdom. Portray-
ing Him subduing his enemies, the prophet says, "And he shall
smite the earth with the rod of his mouth." Hosea 6:5 also
testifies to the power of God's words by saying, "I have slain
them by the words of my mouth." "Word" in this verse is *rhema*
in Greek. This means the spoken word in particular. So the Spirit,
who indwells us, speaks God's Word through us. Of course He
uses the Scriptures as did Jesus when withstanding Satan, the
tempter. "It is written" is the refrain of Christ the Conqueror as
He sounds forth His triumph over the devil (Matt. 4:4, 7, 10).

Two lady missionaries, travelling in a mountainous region of
Mexico, lost their way and were overtaken by darkness. Their
guide proved to be a worthless defender when two desperadoes
attacked them. Literally, in the clutches of one of these villains

for a matter of an hour, the senior missionary audibly called to God in prayer for deliverance. And God enabled her to "withstand in the evil day" until her captor relaxed his hold and released her and thus the party escaped.

Imagine Whitefield preaching to thousands in the open air. How "the word of God" as spoken by him must have been the Spirit's sword laying low hundreds. Hear Jonathan Edwards at Northampton and Enfield so preach from the text, "Their foot shall slide in due time" (Deut. 32:35), that his congregation clings to their seats lest they fall into the pit of hell, so powerful is his word. As one has said, "His was the eloquence of deeply felt thought." See Charles G. Finney enter a village of New York State at nightfall. Urged to preach to the assembled citizens, the revivalist was impressed to relate the biblical account of the Lord destroying Sodom and sparing just Lot. In the midst of his sermon the people began to cry out to God for mercy. Upon Finney's inquiring of some as to the particular occasion of their anxiety he was told that the name of the village was *Sodom* and the only just man in the place was named *Lot*. Yes, God's Word spoken by His servant is accompanied by the unction of the Holy Spirit and is a broadside which Satan cannot resist.

g. THE POWER OF PRAYER (6:18-20).

The several terms used in verses 18-20 provide an interesting study on prayer. "Always" is literally at every seasonable time, *en panti kairo. Kairos* is "time" in the sense of opportunity or season. There are critical times when men instinctively pray to God for supernatural help. Then there are situations, sensed by the spiritually minded, when they realize that only prayer will turn defeat into victory.

"Prayer," *proseuche,* is prayer in general or corporate prayer as offered in the "prayer-meeting." Hence it suggests more formal prayer, including adoration, supplication, and thanksgiving. But "supplication," *deesis,* is earnest, particular petition for some special need in a time of emergency. It is important that prayer be offered "in the Spirit" as the Authorized Version says. The Greek of this is *en pneumati,* in spirit or with spirit. Hence the prayer is to be spiritual or spirited. It is not to emanate merely from the intellect as did that solemn prayer said to be "The most eloquent prayer ever delivered to a Boston audience." Prayers directed to audiences are flimsy weapons with which to combat principalities and powers. Nor should it be a selfish soulish prayer which God may answer but bring leanness to the soul. But let it come from the heart of hearts solemnly but sincerely and unselfishly.

And we are expected to be "watching thereunto with all perseverance and supplication for all saints" (Eph. 6:18). "Watching," *agrypnountes,* means to lie awake and watch and so be intent upon a thing. Some lie awake because they cannot dismiss their business cares or their troubles from their minds. Others lie awake because their duties demand that they refrain from slumber. The mother whose weary body sleeps while her loving heart wakes, the faithful nurse who keeps vigil to cool the fevered brow, these watch with intention by force of will unlike the five foolish virgins who "slumbered and slept." Our watching in prayer is to be characterized by "all perseverance and supplication." Of these words the former comes from *kartos* which means strength that grips or holds on. So persevering prayer is importunate prayer. As Jesus says in Luke 11:10, "For every one who keeps on asking continues to receive, and he who continues to seek keeps on finding, and to him who keeps on knocking it shall be opened." This is the extensity of prayer. Why is this quality of prayer stressed? We seek in vain for an answer to our question in the Bible. But how else can we keep our own receptive faith at white heat than by expressing it? And evidently Jesus advocates importunity which means more than earnestly asking once. It is petition to the point of impudence as *anaidian,* translated "importunity" in Luke 11:8, literally means. As Jesus uttered: "And shall not God avenge his own elect, which cry day and night unto him, though he bear long with them? I tell you that he will avenge them speedily" (Luke 18:7, 8). "Supplication" suggests the intensity of prayer. It represents the outcry of one so needy as to want his prayer answered at once. It is a "now or never" prayer. Such prayer is to be "for all saints." Provincial praying is lacking in Christian compassion.

The writer calls for special, specific supplication for himself. "And for me" he adds to "all saints." This could be rendered "Even for my sake." *Hyper,* "for," suggests substitution, and the apostle asks that the Ephesians' prayers be offered up for his interest as though they were his prayers. Paul pleads for powerful prayer for his public utterances. He knew that the Ephesians knew of his gifts and grace as a speaker. He had been at Ephesus for three years as a teacher and preacher. Yet as he faces "principalities and powers . . . spiritual wickedness in the heavenlies" he desires to have something to say, *logos,* as he opens his mouth to speak. His plea is for boldness, *parresia* (6:19) literally every word or every one speaking. He is "an ambassador in bonds"— literally in a chain, *en halysei.* But the Word must not be bound. "The mystery of the gospel" must be boldly proclaimed. Here is a "freedom" of speech.

Satan's forces would limit the spread of the gospel. They would chain all ambassadors. But this they cannot do if we pray. Luther wrote hymns and translated the Scriptures when in Wartburg Castle; Bunyan wrote *Pilgrim's Progress* while in Bedford jail; Paul wrote Ephesians, Philippians, Colossians, and Philemon when in a Roman prison; he stretched forth his hand and "answered for himself" before King Agrippa when he was a prisoner at Caesarea.

CHAPTER SUMMARY

FACING THE FOE
(Eph. 6:10-20)

We should "be filled with the Spirit," that we "may be able to stand against the wiles of the devil." Hence we are admonished to "put on the whole armour of God."

1. The Strength of Our Foe (vv. 11, 12)

2. "The Whole Armour of God" (vv. 14-20)
   a. The girdle of truth (v. 14a).
   b. The "breastplate of righteousness" (v. 14b).
   c. The shoes of the gospel (v. 15).
   d. The "shield of faith" (v. 16).
   e. The "helmet of salvation" (v. 17a).
   f. The "sword of the spirit" (v. 17b).
   g. Powerful prayer (vv. 18-20)
      (1) Prayer should be continually offered (v. 18a).
      (2) It should include "supplication" (v. 18b).
      (3) It should include "watching" (v. 18c).
      (4) It should be specific (v. 19).
      (5) Such prayer makes for boldness (v. 20).

GREEK WORD STUDIES

An alphabetical index of words found in Ephesians which are studied from the *Greek* text in this volume:

155

BIBLIOGRAPHY

ALFORD, DEAN HENRY. *The Greek New Testament*. London: Rivington, 1861.

BEGBIE, HAROLD. *Twice Born Men*. New York: Fleming H. Revell Co., 1909.

BENSON, CLARENCE H. *An Introduction to Child Study*. Chicago: Moody Press, 1935.

EADIE, JOHN, D.D., L.L.D. *A Commentary on the Greek Text of the Epistle of Paul to the Ephesians*. Clark, 1883, Third edition.

ELLICOTT, C. J. *A Critical and Grammatical Commentary on . . . Ephesians*. Boston: Draper and Halliday, 1867.

ERDMAN, CHARLES. *The Epistle of Paul to the Ephesians*. Westminster Press, 1931.

FARRAR, F. W. *Message of the Books*. New York: E. P. Dutton and Co., 1888.

GREEN, SAMUEL G. *A Handbook of Church History*. New York: Fleming H. Revell Co., 1904.

HARRISON, NORMAN B. *His Love*. Minneapolis: Harrison Service.

Lange's Commentary on Ephesians. Translations and additions by M. B. RIDDLE, D.D. New York: Charles Scribner's Sons, 1879.

MOULTON AND MILLIGAN. *Vocabulary of the Greek New Testament*. London: Hodden and Stoughton, 1930, one volume edition.

MULLINS, E. Y. *Why is Christianity True?* Philadelphia: American Baptist Publication Society, 1905.

MEYER, F. B. *Through the Bible Day By Day*. American Sunday School Union, c. '14, '16, '17, '18.

MEYER, F. B. *Tried By Fire*. New York: Fleming H. Revell Co.

NESTLE, EBERHARD, D.D. *The New Testament in Greek*.

SEELEY, PROF. JOHN R. *"Ecce Homo."* Boston: Little, Brown and Co., 1867.

SPURGEON, CHARLES. *Autobiography*. American Baptist Society.

THAYER, JOSEPH H. *A Greek-English Lexicon of the New Testament*. American Book Co. Corrected edition of April 10, 1889.

TRENCH, ARCHBISHOP RICHARD C. *Synonyms of the New Testament*. Kegan Paul, 1906.

INDEX

DATE DUE

FEB 7 '86			